FIRE FROM THE SKY
1966 UFO Incident in Edinburg, Texas

By
Noe Torres

RoswellBooks.com

Edinburg, Texas

ISBN 978-1-7342523-1-6

First Edition

Cover art by Jason Moser

Printed in the United States of America

DEDICATION

For the citizens of Edinburg, Texas – one of South Texas' oldest, proudest, and most unique communities. It was where I was born and where most of my most important life moments have happened.

CONTENTS

INTRODUCTION

The year 1966 featured a "wave" of unidentified flying object sightings all over North America and throughout the world. The book you hold in your hands focuses on one, little-known UFO incident that happened in deep South Texas and that only came to light in 2012. It was 46 years after the event that one of the witnesses finally decided to come forward and disclose what he and his father witnessed in 1966. The witnesses had been intimidated by military personnel who advised them never to speak about what they had seen. Since both witnesses had close ties to the military and law enforcement communities, they went along with the cover-up for nearly five decades. It was only after the main witness died and his son retired that the truth finally came out. Although the Edinburg incident is just one of hundreds reported in 1966, we feel it has a number of unique features that make it worthy of further study.

1966 was also the year that the astonishing book *The Interrupted Journey: Two Lost Hours Aboard a Flying*

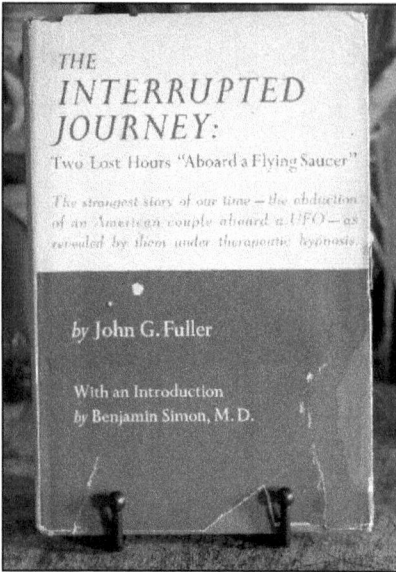

Saucer by John G. Fuller was released to acclaim and instant bestseller status. It told the story of a married couple, Barney and Betty Hill, who claimed they were abducted by extraterrestrials in 1961 in the White Mountains of New Hampshire. The book disclosed that the Hills were chased by a UFO and then forced to go on board, where they were both subjected to medical and scientific experiments by the strange, non-human occupants of the spacecraft. The book, which was the first to deal with alien abduction in a serious, scientific manner, remains one of the most influential in UFO history. The story made the front cover of *Look* magazine in October 1966.

Another book, *Flying Saucers ... Serious Business* by Frank Edwards, also achieved great fame and changed the thoughts of many people who had previously disregarded UFO reports as nonsensical fakery.

Also in 1966, future United States president Gerald Ford sent a letter in his capacity as the House Republican Leader, asking for a Congressional investigation of UFOs. The cover letter said, "Ford is not satisfied with the Air Force explanation of the recent sightings in Michigan and describes the 'swamp gas' version by astrophysicist J. Allen Hynek as 'flippant.'"

The world was changing in 1966, although very slowly, as more and more people were forced to accept the very real possibility that we are being visited by extraterrestrials operating spacecraft that are far beyond our capabilities.

What happened in Edinburg, located near the Texas-Mexico border, is an important case study illustrating why investigating UFOs is such an important endeavor. It was important in 1966, and it is even more so today.

Noe Torres, October 2023

ONE:
THE DEPUTY SHERIFF

The story of a mysterious UFO incident that happened in 1966 near Edinburg, Texas, originated from one of the area's most famous historical figures, Jose R. Ponce (1921-1988). However, the story was not made public until 2012, because Ponce requested that his son, Jose J. Ponce, not disclose the incident until after the dad's death. This is understandable since during this time, people who experienced UFO encounters were typically ridiculed, and they risked losing their professional credibility.

Known by the nickname "Milo," Jose R. Ponce was an extremely influential law enforcement officer and political figure in deep South Texas. He served as a police officer for the city of Edinburg from 1950 to 1957, a deputy sheriff in Hidalgo County, Texas, from 1957 to 1970, and a captain of the County Highway Patrol from 1970 to 1973. In addition, Ponce served as Hidalgo County Commissioner from 1974 to 1981. Also noteworthy was Ponce's impressive military career. During

World War II, he was a member of the U.S. Marine Corps from 1942 to 1945, serving in the South Pacific. He was part of a squadron attached to a dive bomber, which was an aircraft that dove at a steep angle toward its target, usually a ship at sea, and dropped bombs prior to abruptly pulling back up into the sky. Ponce was honorably discharged in 1945.

Typical U.S. Dive Bomber from 1943 (Public Domain)

Ponce's service to the citizens of Hidalgo County is honored by a county park named after him, the J.R. "Milo" Ponce Memorial Park, located in Edinburg at 3516 East Farm to Market Road 2812.

It was in 1966, his ninth year as a deputy sheriff, that the 45-year-old rising star in law enforcement came across something that he could not understand and that he struggled with for the rest of his life – an encounter with what seemed to be an intelligence from beyond our planet.

1966 was part of an era when whistleblowing was not in vogue. In fact, it was destructive of people's careers and sometimes their lives. Deputy Ponce was deeply rooted in a number of institutions that would have looked narrowly upon any talk of unidentified flying objects and extraterrestrials – the U.S. military, the law enforcement community, the county government, the Roman Catholic Church, the American Legion, and the Veterans of Foreign Wars.

Jose R. Ponce (left), circa 1940s, with wife Olga.
(Courtesy Jose J. Ponce)

Despite an insatiable desire to understand what he witnessed in 1966, Ponce kept silent about it. "My dad was told to never speak about what he had seen," his son Jose J. Ponce remembers, "and being a man of his word, he never did." Clearly, as a person who held important positions of responsibility in government and law enforcement, the potential ramifications of disclosing a UFO incident might have been severe indeed.

As will be discussed at length in a later chapter, two men dressed in military uniforms visited the Hidalgo County Sheriff's Department, where Ponce worked, and made it clear that the military did not want any information released to the public about what happened at the Sam Gonzalez Ranch, where the UFO was seen.

Artist's Depiction of UFO (Pixabay)

Deputy Ponce, whose career in law enforcement was on a steep upward trajectory, recognized the wisdom of accepting the order given to him by Sheriff Elmer Elton Vickers. Ponce decided that he would take the story of the UFO case with him to the grave. "No more was ever said of the incident," remembers his son, "and my father never spoke about it anymore."

The only person with whom Ponce discussed the incident in detail was his son, who accompanied him to the scene of the UFO encounter a few hours after it happened. As of the writing of this book, Jose J. Ponce retains a vivid recollection of the unbelievable scene he witnessed of the after-effects of what happened when an unidentified flying object appeared one night and emitted a horrific burst of fire from the sky, causing destruction and nearly the deaths of eight men.

TWO:
SAM GONZALEZ RANCH

Interestingly, the ranch where the UFO incident happened was within 20 miles of where Deputy Jose R. "Milo" Ponce spent part of his youth. Although a native of neighboring Starr County, Ponce and his family moved to the Santa Monica Ranch, about 30 miles northwest of Edinburg, in 1936.

On the night that the UFO incident happened, Deputy Ponce was the one dispatched to the site, which was within his patrol area and with which he was very familiar. In yet another bit of irony, Ponce later served for seven years as the Hidalgo County Commissioner for Precinct 4, which encompasses the Sam Gonzalez Ranch area.

Sam Gonzalez, the owner, was a prominent, civic-minded funeral director from Edinburg. Gonzalez was co-owner of the Ceballos-Diaz Funeral Home in town and was active in local politics and social organizations. Gonzalez was a very close friend of the Ponce family, and Jose J. Ponce remembers spending a lot of time out at the Gonzalez Ranch hunting deer, rabbits, and other game. The Ponce family continued visiting the ranch for years after the incident happened in 1966.

"My dad and Sam were very good friends," Jose J. Ponce remembers, "He used to go out to the ranch quite a lot to hunt deer. I used to go there with him."

To get to the Sam Gonzalez Ranch from downtown Edinburg, one would take U.S. Highway 281 north for twelve miles and then take Farm to Market Road 490 west for two miles.

Years later, the ranch became known for hosting an annual event called "The Panocha Bread Cook-Off," in which cooks attempted to create a historic cowboy-style bread known as "pan de campo."

-0-

IN THE COASTAL BEND, it's known as "pan de campo," or "camp bread." In other parts of the state, it's called "panocha." But whatever you call it, if you can prepare it well, you may be able to pick up a first, second or third-place trophy at the upcoming Panocha Bread Cook-Off Nov. 10 in Hidalgo County.

Panocha is a bread traditionally cooked in the open by cowboys, deer hunters and campers. It resembles a flour tortilla, but is larger and thicker. In some areas, it is served at most backyard cookouts.

The Panocha Cook-off will get under way at 10a.m. at the Sam Gonzalez ranch, located 11 miles north of Edinburg and two miles west off U.S. 281. Registration deadline is 9 a.m. and no entry fee will be charged. Preparations will begin at 9:30 a.m.

Further information on the event, which is sponsored by Ceballo-Diaz Funeral Home of Edinburg, Montalvo-Guerra Insurance Agency in Weslaco and American Legion Post 408 of Edinburg, may be obtained by phoning Thomas Esparza at 383-2285. —D.G.M.

Article About Pan de Campo Annual Event
(10-31-1979, Brownsville Herald)

All along Farm to Market Road 490 were vast stretches of flat, brushy, rocky ranchland, the province of grazing livestock and horses, intermingled with land areas used for oil and gas exploration or mining of caliche, an abundant local resource.

A recent article from the University of Texas – Rio Grande Valley said, "An iconic image of south Texas are pickup trucks roaring down country roads kicking up a 'rooster tail' of white dust. That white dust is 'caliche.' The material occurs naturally throughout the Southwest. Caliche is a sedimentary rock comprised of sand, gravel, clay, and silt cemented together with calcium carbonate. It forms in arid regions like the Rio Grande Valley where the annual precipitation is low."

Aerial View of Caliche Pit at UFO Site
(2018 Photo Courtesy Danny Galeana)

"In the nineteenth century, wells were excavated through layers of caliche and the material was then used to construct *norias* (water wells) and other related structures at ranch sites. Beginning in the twentieth century, caliche was commercially quarried and crushed for use as a base material to improve drainage and traction on unpaved roads. It also was mined and burnt to make quick lime, an ingredient in Portland cement, which was used in the construction of storm sewers and of Falcon Dam."

In 1966, caliche was being excavated out of the ground at the Sam Gonzalez Ranch, as well as other properties along Farm to Market 490. The caliche was likely being used in a number of local construction projects in the area, including the paving of roads.

Caliche and Metal Fragments Strewn Along Wall of the Pit
(2018 Photo Courtesy Danny Galeana)

A Texas ranch owner recently wrote, "In this part of Texas there is a thick layer of caliche running under the topsoil. On my place it starts 9 feet down and is about 21 feet thick.... For those landowners who have a caliche pit it is a revenue source as they sell it to the county, to the state, to road builders and anyone needing a base for concrete slabs."

Jose J. Ponce remembers that in 1966 there were a number of caliche operations going on all around the area of the ranch.

A crew of eight construction workers had brought in trucks and heavy equipment to the Sam Gonzalez Ranch and had set up a temporary camp where the workers lived on site while they engaged in the work for which they had been contracted. Although an exact inventory of what was at the site is unknown, the construction crew had a 12-foot by 60-foot, single wide mobile home in which they slept, two pickup trucks they used to go into town, a bobtail truck, and an excavating machine. In addition, they possibly may have had a bulldozer, a rock crusher, a loader, or a dump truck.

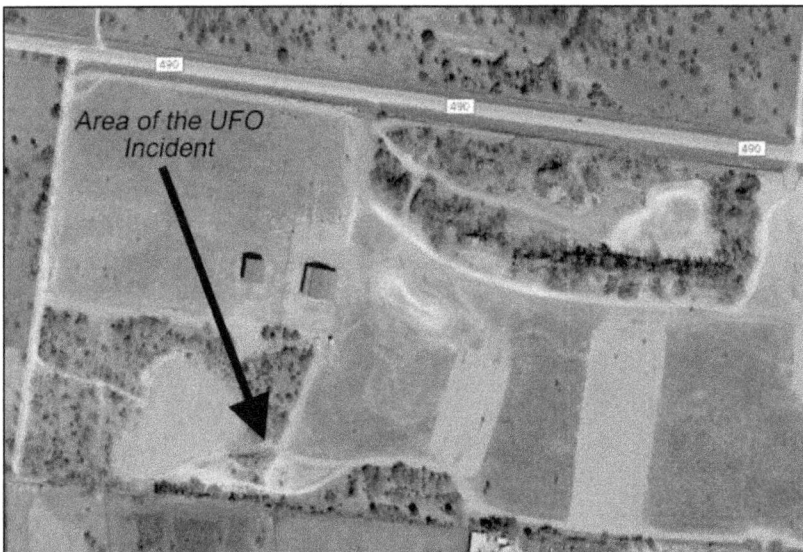

USGS satellite map shows the area of the incident. The decimal coordinates are 26.452163, -98.163800.

Not much is known about the eight men that comprised this work crew. They were all from the area of Dallas, Texas, and were described as "roughneck types," indicating that they were seasoned, hardened construction workers who took a no-nonsense approach to their work and their lives. Given their "rough" exterior, it was therefore telling that they reacted with great horror and fear to the UFO encounter they experienced. Their fear was so great that at least one of these men "wet his pants" during the encounter with the UFO, according to Deputy Ponce who first contacted the men and spent time talking to them about what they saw that evening.

THREE:
FLOATING ORBS

Long before 1966, the area along both sides of Farm to Market Road 490, including the Sam Gonzalez Ranch, was well known to local residents for the frequent appearance of "ghost lights" at nighttime. When Deputy Ponce interviewed the eight construction workers about the UFO incident, they told him that they had previously sighted "glowing orbs" hovering over the fields surrounding their work camp. They also occasionally saw "bright lights" pointing down at the ground from the sky, and they heard "loud humming or throbbing sounds."

A local ranch foreman, known as "Manito," who lived immediately south of where the incident happened, reported seeing a 'cigar-shaped object' that hovered over the fields surrounding the ranch. Manito had seen this type of flying object and bright lights in the sky prior to the night of the 1966 incident, but more importantly, he saw the object on the very night of the incident, as he told the sheriff's deputies that were investigating at the scene.

Deputy Ponce's son, Jose J., remembers, "All of these people that lived out there in the 1960s all reported basically the same thing -- that late at night or sometimes in the early evening, they would see these strange lights in the sky. And apparently that night when the incident occurred, there were strange lights in the sky."

On the day after the incident, Manito rode up on his horse to the site, where he was questioned by sheriff's deputies. Jose J. Ponce said, "And when they asked him about the lights and what he had seen, he simply said that what he had seen was an object that appeared to be cigar shaped, and it was illuminated, and he said that it would light up the field. And it would light up the neighboring brush line... But anyway, on this night, Manito said the lights had been there that night."

Deputy Ponce's Son, Jose J. Ponce, Points to Caliche Pit Where the UFO Incident Happened (2012 Photo)

Other residents along 490 called the eerie night lights "La Luz del Llano," which in English means "the light

16

in the fields." According to Jose J. Ponce, this area has been known for years as the site of strange phenomena.

Another man named Tino, who owned the San Alfonso Bar nearby, stated that he had seen the strange flying lights on many previous occasions. Also witnessing the phenomenon was a nearby resident named Juan Jose Avila, who said he often saw the lights at night, hovering over the local fields. Avila also claimed that one night when the lights came particularly close, a number of random objects in his home "levitated" and began floating in the air. Yet another man, Ramoncito from nearby Faysville, said that while walking on the property of the Sam Gonzalez Ranch, he observed one of the glowing, hovering lights and was approached by it, causing him to feel threatened.

The Edinburg area was not the only place in South Texas where this phenomenon was observed. In a *Brownsville Herald* article from December 11, 1966, these mysterious floating orbs are described in more detail. "Those balls of fire floating around the Valley that now have graduated to the fancy name of unidentified flying objects have been around a long time. At least for 80 years, says Conrado Garcia, the incoming district clerk in Willacy County."

The article continues, "As a matter of fact, these hovering, weaving, and speeding fireballs have been around for so long they figure in the borderland folklore. The fireball is known as *La Luz Errante* (the wandering light) or *La Lampara del Llano* (the lamp of the plains), or *El Farol del Llano*." Other people referred to these lights as "La Luz del Pirate" and believed that they pointed the way to buried treasure.

In the *Brownsville Herald article*, a number of stories are told about these sightings dating as far back as the 1920s. In one story, a man named Natividad Zarate stated that he saw the phenomenon in December 1928: "It was almost red, like the flame of an oil lamp. It weaved around slowly, within a few hundred yards. It flew along and then it split into four separate lights." Another man, Antonio Villarreal, had an eerily similar encounter in 1937.

So, on that fateful Fall evening in 1966, the construction crew from Dallas had already had several sightings of these strange nighttime lights that seemed to be hovering all around their campsite. After the incident, the men told sheriff's deputies that it was not the first time they had seen these eerie lights.

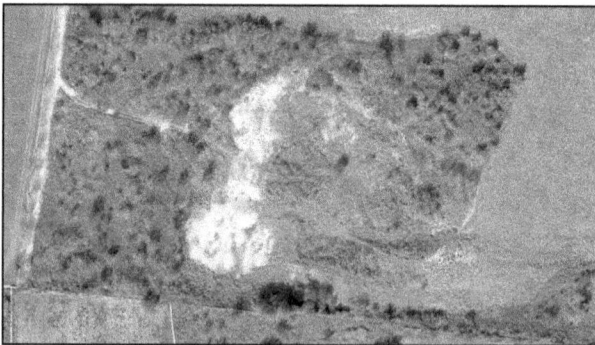

Aerial View of Caliche Pit in 2012

Obviously on the night of the incident, the men were frightened and already on edge due to their previous encounters with the orbs. It was certainly also disconcerting for them to be working in a strange, remote area of the state, far away from their homes. The nights were especially disturbing, since few people resided near their camp, and there were no streetlights or other sources of illumination anywhere near them.

Undoubtedly, the construction workers were very well armed, with both handguns and long guns. Their weapons would help them protect their property, should the need arise, and would also be beneficial for hunting small game out in the wild. In a land well known for a number of unfriendly wild beasts, including rattlesnakes, feral hogs, etc., weapons would be viewed as a much-needed lifeline.

Jose J. Ponce Points to the UFO Site (2012 Photo)

Jose J. Ponce agrees with the idea that the workers would be armed because of all the potential dangers all around them. "Lots of rattlesnakes and other dangerous critters out there," Ponce said. "It doesn't seem likely that those men would be unarmed."

"I can't say for sure that the men fired at that object," Ponce added, "But it certainly seems possible, especially since they were already nervous and on edge from having seen it previously."

Given that the construction workers were likely well-armed, it seems clear that, when a massive UFO appeared over their camp and revealed itself out of a cloud bank, they felt immediately threatened. The men no doubt reached for their weapons, and, as futile as the effort may seem to us today given all we know about UFOs, the men turned their guns upon the rapidly approaching flying saucer. The consequences were devastating, as will be seen in our upcoming chapters.

FOUR:
THE CALL COMES IN

The Edinburg UFO incident happened, according to Jose J. Ponce, either in October or November of 1966. It started at around midnight when the telephone suddenly began ringing at the Ponce residence in Edinburg, at 722 East Fay Street. For Deputy Ponce, who was on call that evening, the ringing of the phone in the middle of the night was not an unexpected occurrence. As he popped out of bed and ambled over to the phone, he was certainly wondering which of the usual scenarios the call would be about.

Typically, the sheriff's office responded to matters such as traffic accidents, escaped livestock, domestic disputes, vandalism, brush fires, theft, and so on. Occasionally, they would get a call about a "crazy person" misbehaving or threatening harm to themselves or others.

When Deputy Ponce picked up the phone, he immediately heard the seasoned voice of George Rapp, veteran dispatcher for the Hidalgo County Sheriff's

Department. A Republican who lived in nearby Mission, Texas, Rapp made a stab at running for sheriff in 1960 but ended up working for the winner of the race, Elmer Elton Vickers (1889-1971), known as "E. E."

Deputy Ponce (far right) and Sheriff Vickers (2nd from left)
Courtesy Jose J. Ponce

On that evening in 1966, dispatcher Rapp stated that someone had called the office to report a group of "disturbed men" standing alongside Farm to Market Road 490. According to the report, the eight "Anglo" men were standing alongside the road yelling and screaming at the occasional vehicle that passed by them at such a late time of night. It remains unclear to this day exactly who made the call to the sheriff. It may have been a passing motorist who later stopped at a local residence or business to call the authorities. Or, it may have been one of the few people who lived in the area at that time.

After dispatcher Rapp described what was happening out on 490, Deputy Ponce was a bit taken aback by the information. "Is this serious?" Ponce asked, "Or is this some kind of prank call?" Rapp responded by stating that the eight "disturbed" men appeared to be very frightened by whatever they had witnessed and were also saying to passing motorists that they needed help putting out a fire.

Hanging up with Rapp, Deputy Ponce got dressed, got in his patrol vehicle, a white, 4-door Studebaker, and responded to the call as instructed.

Studebaker Police Car, Typical of the 1960s

Upon arriving at the scene, Ponce's patrol car was surrounded by eight "agitated" men, all waving their arms wildly and talking at the same time. Although Ponce at first had trouble understanding what they were saying about lights in the sky and fire coming down out of the sky, he quickly picked up that there was a fire in progress at the workers' camp just a short distance away.

He noticed that one of the construction workers had wet his pants. "My dad told me that he had urinated in his pants," Jose J. Ponce remembers. This made quite an impression on Deputy Ponce, because the men seemed to be extremely tough and rugged individuals that would not frighten easily. It seemed totally outside their "roughneck" persona to experience such fear.

Picking up his police radio, Ponce requested additional assistance, including fire trucks. He possibly called it in as a "brush fire." As the construction workers continued talking to him and among themselves, it seemed clear to Deputy Ponce that their camp and all their vehicles and equipment were on fire.

Without doubt, Ponce's curiosity about what happened continued growing as the men raved on with a wild story about an object that came out of the clouds and shot beams of light down at their camp.

Just as the deputy was about to settle the men down and try to get the whole story out of them, he received another surprise. Speaking with one voice, the men insisted on being immediately taken away from the vicinity of the Sam Gonzalez Ranch.

Jose J. Ponce Shows Burned Metal Fragments That Still Litter the UFO Site (2012 Photo)

Although Jose J. Ponce does not know for sure, he believes that his dad probably decided to resume his interview with the men at the Sheriff's Department in Edinburg, rather than trying to continue out at the ranch, with their "disturbed" condition being what it was. Deputy Ponce likely had the men wait out by his patrol car while he walked closer to their camp, which by now was fully engulfed in flames.

Firefighters eventually arrived at the scene, but according to Deputy Ponce, by the time they got there, the flames had mostly died out. The scene was a chaos of smoldering ruins. The horrendous aftermath of the UFO encounter was very apparent to everyone surveying the scene.

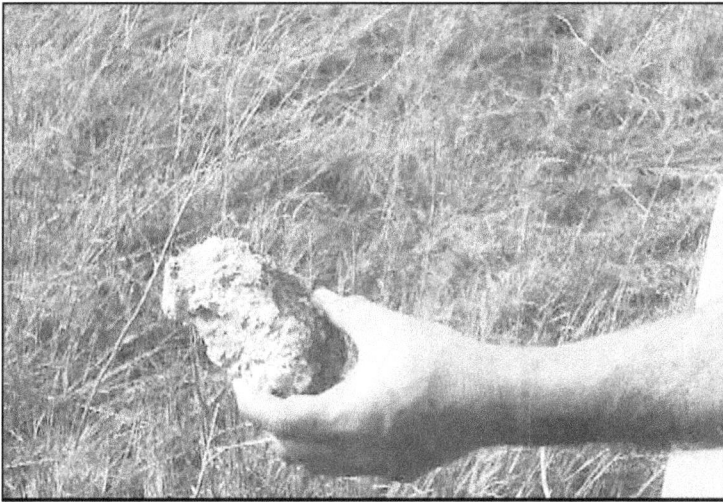

Caliche Rock with Burn Marks at UFO Site, 2012 Photo

Turning from the devastation, Ponce focused on getting the construction workers back to the station in order to hear their full story and get it down in writing. The men crowded into two patrol cars and rambled east on FM 490, headed toward downtown Edinburg. As Ponce and the men left the scene, the firefighters continued to work on completely extinguishing the few remaining flames and keeping the fire contained to within the one caliche pit where it had apparently broken out.

FIVE:
THE WITNESSES SPEAK

It seems certain that the construction workers riding in the patrol car with Deputy Ponce continued talking about what happened to them all the way to the sheriff's office, which in 1966 was located on the first floor of the Hidalgo County Courthouse at 100 N. Closner Boulevard. Since the workers were in a highly agitated state, they likely spent most of the drive to the courthouse discussing what they had seen back at the construction site.

All this discussion came together with the written statements that the men later gave at the sheriff's office to paint a very clear picture of the UFO incident. Everything was written down in the official report of the case, which unfortunately later disappeared from the sheriff's office, as will be discussed in a future chapter.

The construction workers' story begins with a routine day of toil in the excavation of caliche from the pits at the Sam Gonzalez Ranch. After putting in their day, the men settled down for a calm, restful evening in the 12-

foot x 60-foot mobile home that the crew was using as their home base.

The workers told deputies that as they were sleeping, they were suddenly awakened by strong, gusty winds that were so intense that the structure of their mobile home was shaking. They were puzzled by the sounds they heard outside, especially since earlier in the evening they had noticed that the wind was calm, and no threat of storms seemed apparent.

Typical 12' x 60' Trailer Park of the 1960s

As they stepped outside their mobile home, the workers saw a sight that further astonished them. Although all the skies for miles around them were clear and calm, the area immediately above their camp was becoming a roiling cauldron of turbulence. A strange cloud formation had appeared overhead, and within the clouds, the workers could see strange, multicolored lights flashing and shining.

This disturbing sight was punctuated by a loud throbbing or pulsating sound that seemed to vibrate through the men's bodies with a ferocious intensity. They continued looking up as the weather disturbance began to define itself into a cigar-shaped, illuminated object of immense size hovering above their campsite, still partially wrapped in the cloud formation.

Recent Media Event at the UFO Encounter Site
(Courtesy Daniel Jones)

The author has spoken to many witnesses that have had an up-close encounter with one of these otherworldly craft, and the reaction of shock and momentary paralysis is universal. To suddenly behold something that is clearly from outside our known universe has an effect on the human psyche that seems to temporarily remove us from the normal plane of everyday existence. We are moved almost into an alternate dimension, in which all the physical truths we have known since coming out of the womb are turned on their heads. The laws of physics drilled into us during our schooling seem to no longer apply. Pounding in our brain is the realization that we have not been told the truth.

Artistic Conception of a UFO (Pexels)

As the construction workers cowered in fear below this monstrous apparition, the author believes one or more of them scrambled for a weapon. It stands to reason that the men felt incredibly threatened as they later related to the deputies and anybody who would listen. The men's fear and foreboding would certainly have led them to fire their weapons at the object hovering over their heads, hoping to drive the threat off from their camp, it would seem. The reaction they got from the strange object terrified them even more.

What happened next has been the subject of much speculation by quite a number of UFO experts. The hovering craft emitted beams of light down to the construction camp below, bathing all the vehicles, machinery, and the mobile home in an eerie light. Moments later, the light beams turned into beams of fire, which incinerated, for the most part, the mobile home, the crew's pick-up trucks, their bobtail truck, and their excavating machine.

Charred, Twisted Metal from Wreckage (2018 Photo)

As the horrified construction workers turned and fled for their lives, the beams of fire from the sky continued to turn their encampment into a sizzling pit of burned and molten metal. "It was all charred," remembers Jose J. Ponce, who visited the site with his dad on the following day, "All that stuff had been burned."

Most investigators believe that the UFO attacked the campsite only after the construction workers demonstrated aggression by firing their weapons at it. The craft, whether piloted by living beings or by some kind of artificial intelligence, might have had a defense mechanism that sprang to life when hostile actions were detected against it.

Other investigators have suggested that the UFO was not retaliating toward the men, but rather was engaging its engines in preparation for blasting away from the site. At the point where it turned to zoom away, the blast from its propulsion systems incinerated the camp and all the equipment in it.

Yet another theory is that all of the metal structures in the camp (mobile home, pickup trucks, etc.) were affected by forces being generated by the UFO. The proponents of this theory point out that of all the material in the camp, it was mostly the metals that were impacted.

Regardless of what caused the destruction or how, the construction workers did not wait to find out. They ran like wild men for about a quarter mile out to Farm to Market Road 490, where they began to act like the highly disturbed individuals that were later reported to the sheriff's department.

All eight construction workers were interviewed after being taken to the sheriff's office. Deputy Ponce and several other deputies were involved in the questioning. By the time the interviews finished, it was very late, and someone offered to take the men to a local hotel for the night or out to the construction site to see if anything was salvageable. Although the men had calmed down to a great degree by this point, the idea of leaving the sheriff's department seemed to once more send them into fear and panic.

They seemed aghast at the notion of returning to the Sam Gonzalez Ranch. "We never want to see that place again," one of the men said. "We are taking a bus in the morning and never coming back here again."

Then they asked the deputies if they might be permitted to stay at the sheriff's office so they could get a few hours of sleep prior to leaving town on the first bus to Dallas. The deputies allowed them to sleep in the jail cells. As far as Deputy Ponce knew, the men left Edinburg the next morning and never returned to South Texas.

SIX:
THE DAY AFTER

On the following morning, Deputy Ponce, his son Jose J., and another deputy drove out to the site of the previous night's UFO incident, intent on assessing the damage to the construction camp. What they found totally astonished them. The fire had not merely burned the mobile home, vehicles, and equipment, it had totally destroyed everything, leaving only burned husks and scraps of metal.

Twisted, Burned Metal Wreckage (2012 Photo)

The 12-foot x 60-foot mobile home was completely gutted, turned into a burned skeleton, surrounded by twisted vines of metal. The crew's two pick-up trucks looked like bombs had hit them, with only the burned-out frames remaining. Also completely gutted were the bobtail truck and the excavating machine.

For Deputy Ponce and his son, the devastation was not the end of the matter. The UFO incident continued to weigh heavily on their minds for many years afterward. When visiting the Sam Gonzalez Ranch, they would occasionally go to the burn site to rummage through the remains and try to make sense of what happened.

For years afterward, they remembered the desperate pleas for understanding from the construction workers. Jose J. Ponce recites the troubling part of the story, "Something had come out of the clouds in the night sky and had directed a beam of fire down at their camp. They saw flames shooting down out of the sky, setting ablaze all of the surrounding area, including their vehicles and their mobile home."

Jose J. moved to Louisiana in 1967 and was gone from Edinburg until 1972, but upon his return, he and his dad went out to look at the UFO site. Even though six years had passed, Jose J. remembers that the evidence of what happened that night was still easy to find. He said, "Years later, after I returned ... in 1972, I visited the area with my father. He pointed out the location and you could still see an oddly shaped area where nothing would grow. The sides of the pit appeared to have been burned all the way to the top, 25 to 30 feet high."

His statement that "nothing would grow" is interesting in the context of other UFO encounters, in which the landing or close approach of a flying saucer radically affects the nearby soil and vegetation. In many UFO landing cases, for example, all vegetation at the spot where the craft touched down is often said to no longer grow for long periods of time. The thought is that some type of radiation or electromagnetic forces from the craft have impacted the soil that surrounded the landing zone.

Ben Moss and Tony Angiona (at front with backs turned) and others at the UFO site in 2019.

UFO experts Ben Moss & Tony Angiona, who visited the site in 2019, scanned the surrounding area of the caliche pit with Geiger counters and electromagnetic field (EMF) meters. They detected several anomalous readings indicating slightly higher than normal radioactivity and also elevated EMF signatures.

There was one particular piece of twisted metal that seemed to have a significantly high EMF reading, according to Moss and Angiona. Although the readings were not completely off the charts, they were of sufficient intensity to raise the eyebrows of the assembled spectators at the UFO site in 2019.

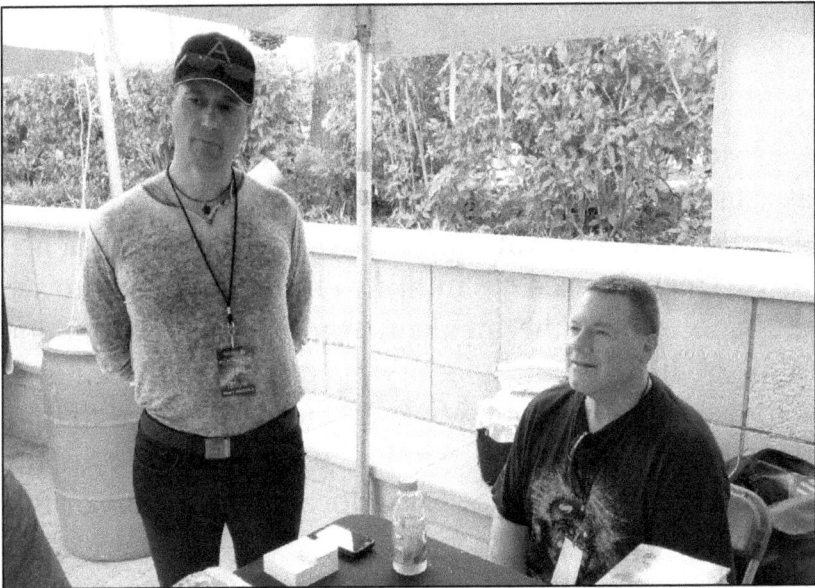

Tony Angiona (left) and Ben Moss (right) during 2019 Edinburg visit

SEVEN:
THE COVERUP BEGINS

Jose J. Ponce says that Sheriff E. E. Vickers and his assistant, Tom Wingert, told his dad that, shortly after the 1966 Edinburg incident, they had been approached by two men dressed in "military uniforms" asking to see the report about the incident. Apparently, Vickers and Wingert had trouble identifying exactly what kind of uniform the men wore. Vickers later told Ponce that he thought they might be Air Force men because of the nearby Moore Air Force Base, located northwest of Edinburg.

The problem with Vickers' theory is that Moore Air Base had been closed by the Air Force in 1961 and was no longer a military institution at the time of the Edinburg UFO incident. Even though the base had been closed and turned over to the U.S. Department of Agriculture for its Screwworm Eradication Program, military aircraft still did occasionally land and take off from there. It's possible that Air Force investigators, perhaps from Wright-Patterson Air Force Base near Dayton,

Ohio, arrived by plane at Moore Air Base and then proceeded by car to the sheriff's office in Edinburg.

It was obviously the job of these two men to make sure that the "paper trail" generated by the UFO incident at the Sam Gonzalez ranch would disappear, along with the hopes of members of the public wanting to know exactly what happened there. Several UFO researchers, including this author, have spent many hours since 2012 looking for the smallest scrap of data to confirm Deputy Jose R. Ponce's story. We have checked with the sheriff's department and with the Edinburg Fire Department, which would have responded to the fire, but absolutely no records remain.

In addition to the documents disappearing, it seems clear that the military went out to the Sam Gonzalez Ranch shortly after the incident and combed the place for anything that might be construed as evidence of a UFO visitation.

Aerial View of UFO Site (2018 Photo)

Over the years, as investigators have searched through the rubble and debris that is still scattered throughout the caliche pit site, evidence has been found that a large group of people, probably a military detail, worked at the site, most likely immediately after the 1966 incident.

Military-style jacket found partially buried at UFO site.

In 2017, the family that currently owns the ranch, found buried in the dirt what appears to be a military jacket from the time period in question (1960s).

The military men who arrived after the Edinburg UFO incident carried out their mission with deadly efficiency. First, they secured all records pertaining to the incident and its aftermath. Chief among those records were the names, addresses, and written eyewitness accounts of the eight construction workers from North Texas. Second, the military undoubtedly went to the Sam Gonzalez Ranch and examined the site thoroughly looking for anything unusual that might promote the belief that a UFO incident had occurred there. And third, the military men in charge of "sanitizing" the case spoke to the law enforcement officials to ensure that they would remain quiet about the case.

UFO Researcher John Greenewald examines the jacket in 2018.

Regarding the possible origin of the jacket, UFO researcher Ruben J. Uriarte said, "Check the left lapel of the jacket. You will see a symbol of an eagle on top of a globe with an anchor. It is Marine Corps. The strip on each sleeve looks like the rank of a private." Also, the style of the jacket definitely matches the time period of the 1960s.

Assuming that the coverup operation was initiated by the U.S. Air Force, the presence of a Marine Corps private helping to clean up the UFO site indicates a multi-agency approach. Some UFO investigators argue that, for these types of clandestine operations, soldiers are drawn seemingly at random from many branches of the military. The thinking is that these individual soldiers will be quickly returned to their units scattered throughout the world and will have less of a chance to question what happened to them.

EIGHT: CONSPIRACY OF SILENCE

Hidalgo County Sheriff Elmer Elton Vickers certainly seems to have been complicit in the government coverup of the Edinburg UFO incident. Deputy Ponce

told his son that two men dressed in military uniforms came to see the sheriff, after which the lid of secrecy slammed down on the sheriff's department. The men asked Vickers for all reports and documents related to the incident at the Sam Gonzalez Ranch. It seems clear that he turned everything over to them and became a willing co-conspirator in making the UFO case "disappear."

There was actually a precedent to Vickers' seemingly reprehensible behavior. The sheriff, a few years prior to the UFO incident, had allegedly helped cover up the 1960 murder of a young schoolteacher in McAllen, Texas, by a Roman Catholic priest named John Feit. Vickers who "assisted" local police with the murder case and promised to "leave no stone unturned" in finding Irene Garza's killer, has been accused of doing exactly the opposite. As a practicing Catholic himself, Vickers has been accused in recent years of impeding and obstructing the Garza murder investigation to provide an opportunity for the killer priest to be transferred away from South Texas and be absorbed in the massive tendrils of the church.

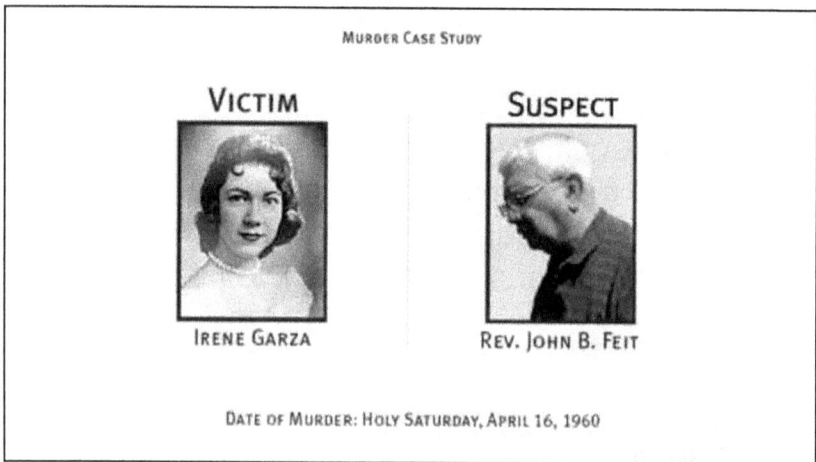

MURDER CASE STUDY

VICTIM

SUSPECT

IRENE GARZA

REV. JOHN B. FEIT

DATE OF MURDER: HOLY SATURDAY, APRIL 16, 1960

From Justice for Irene Facebook

Many years later, investigators uncovered a letter in which a Catholic Church leader stated that Sheriff Vicker's assistance had been "invaluable" in keeping the scandalous murder from hurting the church. The letter read in part, "The sheriff ... also is a Catholic, and he also stands to lose materially by such a scandal here, in such a non-Catholic area. I feel that he has rendered us an invaluable service."

The letter acknowledges a number of recommendations that Vickers made to the church, chief of which was for the murderer to be removed from South Texas as soon as possible, preferably to an overseas post. The church heeded Vickers' advice, and John Feit, the only suspect in the case, vanished to remote Catholic missions, where he thrived for over 50 years.

Feit did not face consequences for his evil deed until 2017, when, at the age of 85, he was found guilty of strangling Irene Garza to death and was convicted to life in prison. Feit died in a prison hospital in 2020.

Thus, it stands to reason that when Sheriff Vickers was faced with a case involving an unidentified flying object in 1966, rather than risk his career and his standing in the community, he possibly may have chosen to slam the door on the case and make no effort at all to find the truth.

NINE:
MOORE AIR BASE

If the military officers that persuaded Sheriff Vickers to "erase" the UFO story did come from nearby Moore Air Base, it would not be a surprise to many local residents. The air base has had a strange history that is shrouded in mystery and secrecy. Many believe that the government may have used the base to test experimental aircraft in the 1950s, 1960s, and possibly even more recently. They point to the fact that nuclear materials were present on the base as early as the mid-1950s. Could these nuclear materials have been used to conduct tests of advanced propulsion systems?

These converted aircraft buildings on the former Moore Air Force Base near Mission, Texas, house the sterile screwworm production plant that is the heart of the Southwest Screwworm Eradication Program. Aircraft in the foreground distribute flies reared in the plant.

Moore Air Base in 1962 (USDA Photo)

In 2005, when the federal government ordered a clean-up of nuclear materials at the base, most observers thought these materials were the miniscule quantities used to irradiate flies during the U. S. Department of Agriculture's Screwworm Eradication Program, which began in 1961. But actually, this was not the case. The Federal Register (April 18, 2006) confirms that there were nuclear materials present at the base as early as the mid-1950s, while the base was under the control of the U. S. Air Force. This was clearly prior to the start of the Screwworm Eradication Program, although government documents claim that the nuclear materials were under the control of the Department of Agriculture "for research and development purposes." Most likely, the materials were actually under the control of the Air Force, and the USDA angle was a cover.

Contaminated materials were buried in and around Moore Air Base. The contamination was severe enough that a "remediation" of the site was ordered in 2005 and subsequently carried out at the base. In the government documents relating to the radioactive clean-up of Moore Air Base (MAB), several unusual sites are noted, including "Site 6," which is described as follows:

2.4 Site 6 Description

Site 6 is referred to, colloquially, as the "Unknown Radioactive Burial Site". In correspondence dated October 31, 1983, the location of this burial appeared to be approximately 800 feet north and 800 feet west from the southeast corner post of the MAB perimeter fence.[12] These materials were originally placed in a four-foot-deep bulldozer excavation, covered with dirt, and then packed down using the same bulldozer.

From 1953 to 1959, Moore Air Base was a primary pilot training center for the U.S. Air Force. Approximately 4,000 pilots were trained, using T28, T34, and T37 aircraft. But in addition to its training functions, the base was no doubt also involved in other less public efforts to gain the upper hand on the Soviet Union during these critical years of the Cold War. The testing of experimental aircraft and experimental propulsion systems could very easily have taken place in such a remote location that was well out of the public view.

An Air Force T-37 flies along the Texas-Mexico border (USAF Photo Archives)

A number of notable pilots received their training at Moore Air Base, including NASA astronaut Al Worden. Before being chosen to the astronaut corps in 1966, Worden received pilot training at the base. He went on to become the command module pilot for Apollo 15 (July 26 - August 7, 1971). It was the fourth manned lunar landing mission. Apollo 15 is notable for being the first to use a lunar roving vehicle, and Worden was the first command module pilot to go on a "spacewalk" outside his vehicle.

Local historian David Newton remembers talking to many of the Air Force pilots that flew in and out of Moore Air Base. Pilots told him they often saw strange, unexplained lights flying around in the vicinity of the base. Newton said, "We have … an area that has been noted for strange lights … frequently mentioned by both trainers and trainees at Moore Field when it was an advanced pilot training facility for the United States Air Force. We knew of various such trainers and other Air Force personnel who lived in McAllen and would mention the odd 'moving lights' when they were on night training missions. These men, frequently combat veterans from WWII or Korea, would suggest at times that they felt as if they were being monitored by intelligently operated craft of unknown origin, sometimes during the day but usually at night."

Moore Air Base (2005 Photo by Noe Torres)

Several former employees of the base have stated that they witnessed strange goings-on while employed there. Gilberto Acosta, Jr., who worked at the base in the early 1980s, said, "On one occasion, a plane landed and five or six men, all dressed in white, covered head to toe, got off the plane. I thought that was rather odd, so I sneaked into the building to see what was going on. I was never able to find any of them. Which made me think there was something going on underground. At that time there were not a lot of people working at the base, just a few skeleton crews. I asked a person about the plane and his comment was, 'What plane? No planes land here.' I just left it at that. Several hours later while I was taking samples in a field, I saw the plane leave."

Moore Air Base (2006 Photo by USGS)

On January 19, 2009, a mysterious fire broke out at Moore Air Base and quickly spread over 2,500 acres, partially destroying four hangars at the base and threatening dozens of nearby homes. Afterward, federal authorities said the blaze was caused by an electrical failure. According to the official explanation, electrical wiring inside one of the hangars at the base failed, igniting a wildfire that caused $10 million in damage at the base. Skeptics, however, wonder how such a large fire could have resulted from a simple wiring problem.

In March 2012, a very eerie UFO incident happened within three miles of Moore Air Base. An eyewitness saw a very strange craft hovering over a nearby road. Could it have been an unconventional aircraft being tested by the military?

Natalie, whose last name is withheld, was the eyewitness who was driving her car north on Conway Road, about halfway between State Highway 107 and Monte Christo Road, when she saw the craft hovering about 30 feet above the roadway. This happened at approximately 3:30 a.m. to Natalie, a housewife in her mid-40s who worked at a non-profit agency in nearby Edinburg.

She was driving in the area because she had noticed a very bright light shining through the kitchen window of her home near the intersection of Freddy Gonzalez Drive and Jackson Road in Edinburg. She saw the light after having trouble sleeping and getting up for a drink of water.

Looking out her kitchen window to the northwest, she saw an intensely bright light hovering above the horizon. Thinking it was much nearer to her home than it actually was, Natalie decided to get in her car and drive toward the light, which ended up being a drive of approximately ten miles.

When she approached the vicinity of Moore Air Base, driving north on Conway Road, she finally could see the cause of the intensely bright light. It was a large, saucer-shaped craft hovering about 30 feet above the asphalt and having a clearly visible wind effect on nearby brush and trees.

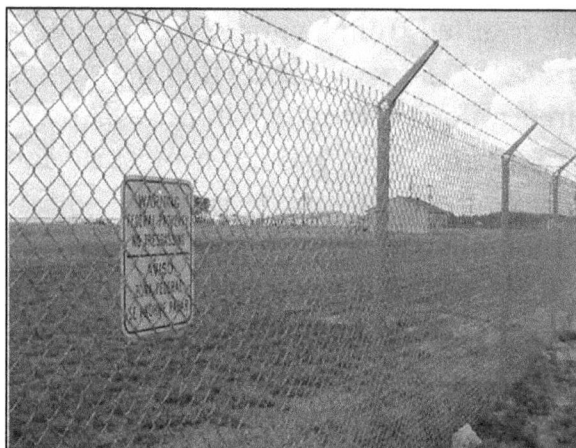

Moore Air Base (2005 Photo by Noe Torres)

Standing by the roadblock were two "highway patrolmen," who were also turned toward the strange object and were staring at it intently. Getting out of her car, Natalie approached the officers, while continuing to look at the UFO. She turned to one of the patrolmen and asked, "Are you seeing what I'm seeing."

The officer replied, "Yes, ma'am" and then advised her that she was not allowed to remain there and had to leave immediately. She complied with these instructions, but not before turning and looking one last time at the amazing sight of the UFO that hovered just beyond the police roadblock.

There remain many questions regarding the 1966 Edinburg UFO Incident and what role, if any, Moore Air Base has had in the numerous UFO sightings that have been reported over the years in and around the base. During a recent visit to the base, this author approached one of the guards at the entrance to the base and requested to take photos inside the base. "No, you can't do that," was his immediate response.

"If we see you taking photographs while standing on this property, we will have to arrest you," he said. Clearly, the government is not interested in giving up any of its secrets anytime soon.

TEN:
THEORIES

Regarding the strange craft from which the fire came, some researchers have speculated that it might have been a type of experimental aircraft being flown out of Moore Air Base, about ten miles away. During a visit in April 2018 to the site of the fire, Stephen Bassett, founder of Paradigm Research Group, said, "We know that during this time period, the fifties and sixties, the military was making crude efforts to reproduce some of the aerial capabilities that were being observed in UFOs."

UFO expert Stephen Bassett (left) with author Noe Torres at the site of the 1966 Edinburg Incident

"If what happened here in Edinburg involved one of these, what I call, Alien Reproduction Vehicles (ARP), it's possible that it was unstable and may have discharged some kind of energy down to the surface below, causing everything around here to combust."

"This could be another Cash-Landrum scenario [a 1980 UFO case in East Texas where a suspected ARP caused eyewitnesses to become ill with radiation poisoning from a close encounter with the craft]," Bassett added. "This ship seen here in Edinburg could be an Alien Reproduction Vehicle, an early attempt that was unstable and that triggered an electrical discharge from the craft down to the ground."

"Think of it as an ARP that is using some type of energy system for propulsion, which is generating a very powerful electric field around it. It got too low and discharged down to the ground, striking everything that was metal here in this field and blowing it up."

John Greenewald, founder of the Internet site *The Black Vault*, said that it is no surprise to him at all that Air Force personnel would have come in after the Edinburg case to put a lid on it, making sure that no information about the incident leaked out to the general public.

During a 2018 visit to the site, Greenewald said, "It's not surprising that they would arrive on site, take all the files generated by law enforcement, and make it all disappear. That is how we see them operate in case after case." He added that the files may have been taken to Wright-Patterson Air Force Base near Dayton, Ohio, where he believes most highly classified UFO documents are kept.

John Greenewald (right) at Edinburg UFO Site

In addition to making the documents disappear, Stephen Bassett believes that a squad of soldiers was sent out to the site of the fire to make sure that no telling evidence was left behind of the strange craft's presence in the area. "They obviously sent a team out here," he said, "Although they didn't have to do a full clean up as happened in Roswell, because there was no crash of a vehicle here. However, they did send some men to look things over and quiet everything down."

Military-style jacket found partially buried at UFO site.

Bassett's comments go along with the 2017 discovery at the site of a military-style jacket that appears to date back to the 1960s. The current owner of the ranch said that workers at the ranch spotted the jacket mostly buried in the soil at the former caliche pit. She had the jacket carefully removed, cleaned, and now keeps it as a memento of the 1966 UFO incident.

Regarding the apparent government cover-up of the Edinburg Incident, Nick Pope, the former principal UFO investigator for the British government, said, "There is no getting away from the fact, however you spin it, this was a UFO incident, and as such, the military will respond, as they usually respond. The default position of the military is usually to say nothing, particularly since we are dealing with the era before the Freedom of Information Act, which made it easier to get away with it back then – more so than it would be now."

British UFO expert Nick Pope (left)

While visiting the Edinburg site in April 2018, Pope added, "I think any time you've got an incident like this with the local sheriff's department involved and the military involved, even if things are confiscated, there will be a document trail that researchers to this day may still be able to follow."

"The most fascinating part of this 1966 incident is that [signaling at the area around him] here we are – we can still visit ground zero. There is the possibility of literally doing fieldwork right here, boots on the ground. There may be some residual trace evidence, forensic traces, soil samples, metal detection – so maybe some more evidence can be turned up here."

"The other thing to do, parallel with the field work, is to reach out to the local community. People who have been here for several generations may have heard stories from the old timers about what happened here," Pope said. "Maybe somebody has up in their attic a box of mementos about what happened here, like documents and photos. That's why it's important to make an appeal to the local community for folks to come forward with anything they may have heard or seen regarding this case."

Another interesting angle to this incident is the strange beam of fire that is said to have incinerated everything at the work camp. Travis Walton, who was struck by an energy beam from a UFO prior to being abducted in an Arizona forest in 1975, also visited the Edinburg site in 2018 and commented on the beam that hit him.

The beam that struck Walton was obviously of a different character than the beam that set fire to everything at the Edinburg construction site back in 1966. "The beam that hit me was described by the other witnesses as looking like a sudden, abrupt, explosive burst of lightning or electricity, perhaps a laser beam or energy beam of some kind," Walton said.

UFO abductee Travis Walton (right)

He does not believe the beam was a hostile act on the part of the UFO occupants. "I was not a threat to them. I had no weapons. I was just one guy standing there, posing no threat at all. I believe the beam was some kind of accidental discharge. Before it hit me, I felt like an electrical charge slowly building up in the air around me. Some of the other crewmembers felt it, too. That may have been a type of energy that was building up in the craft itself. Maybe the propulsion system was charging up prior to taking off."

"In the case of the beam that struck here in Edinburg, maybe the energy release caused some flammable things to explode here at the site, like fuel or other flammables, which would then trigger an explosion, fire, and flames. Again, it could have been unintended. It could have just been a side effect of some type of energy from the craft."

ELEVEN:
EVENT AT THE RANCH

THE EDINBURG ARTS FOUNDATION
INVITES YOU TO THE

1966 EDINBURG UFO EVENT

AT THE ORIGINAL ENCOUNTER SITE

On the evening of March 30, 2017, the Edinburg Arts Foundation sponsored the first ever event commemorating the 1966 UFO incident, held at the original site. Author Noe Torres and eyewitness Jose J. Ponce gave a presentation to the large crowd at one of the ranch buildings, and after the presentation, the members of the crowd were encouraged to walk down to the caliche pit with Torres and Ponce. What follows is the transcript of the night's events, with minimal editing. Unless otherwise noted, the speaker is Noe Torres.

We're going to talk about this very strange incident that happened here in 1966 - just behind the barn. Those of you that would like to go and feel able to…. It's quite a hike down to the end of the fence line. We'll be walking, and anybody that wants to go with us, after our short presentation is done. We wanted to get it in before it gets, you know, really dark. So, anybody that wants to come along and stand there and see … We found some of the pieces of the machinery and the mobile home that were destroyed that night, we think. And so, we'll take you out there walking in just a few minutes.

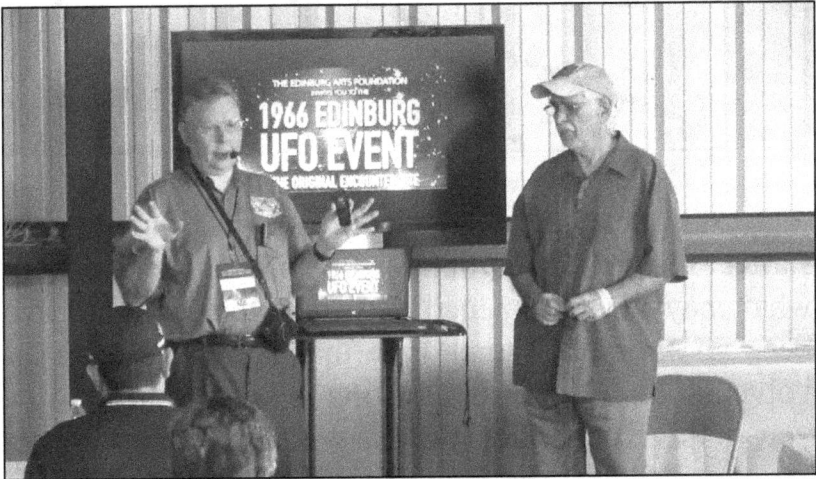

Torres (left) and Ponce (right) presenting at the event.

So, I want to introduce first of all, the gentleman that brought this story to my attention and that's Mr. Joe Ponce. Joe, stand up. Joe's involvement is that his dad, Milo Ponce, was the Hidalgo County Sheriff's deputy that responded to the call that night in 1966 that something strange had happened out here.

There were eight eyewitnesses to this event, and they all told Deputy Ponce what had happened. They were extremely frightened. And we're going to get more into detail on the story as we go along, and I'm going to call on Joe, as we go through the slideshow to give us a little more comment.

So, the location is where we're at now. Before we get started, I want to point out that one of the theories about what may have happened here was there might have been an aircraft of some type that may have been involved in this. What's interesting is I just want to show you, in this first aerial view, that we are not very far from Moore Air Base. About eight aerial miles. Here's where we are right now, and here's Moore Air Base, which, in 1966, was no longer a military base. It had been transferred from the US Air Force to the US Department of Agriculture for the Screwworm Eradication Program, but its runways and hangars were still being maintained, and it was still being used for military aircraft takeoffs and landings. So just keep that in mind that we are kind of in one of the flight paths for Moore Air Base.

Now, here's another interesting thing about out here. This [on the map] is Moore airfield. And right about here is where we are today. This [on the map] is Farm to Market 490. Auxiliary landing field #1 for Moore Air Base is what is now the Edinburg Municipal Airport and also the racetrack. So, that was air base auxiliary landing field #1 for Moore Air Base in the 1940s, 50s and 60s. They also had auxiliary landing field #2, which was northwest of here or northwest of Moore Air Base, and they had auxiliary airfield #3.

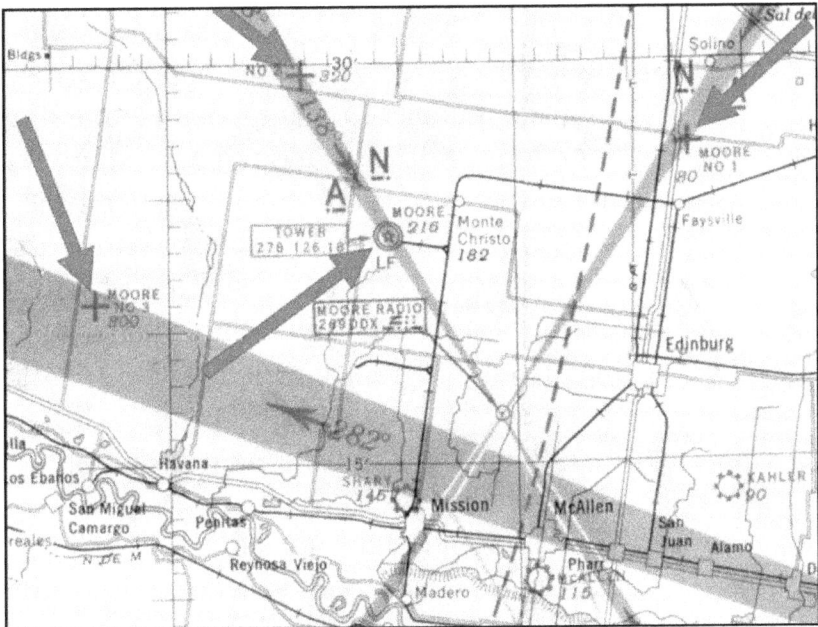

1945 Aviation Chart for Moore Air Force Base

I'm going to talk a little bit later on about some strange stuff that happened with Moore Air Base over the years. It's been one of the former US Air Force bases where a lot of strange activity has been reported over the years and even recently.

So, what happened here on that night in 1966, there was a group of construction workers from North Texas that were down here working on the caliche pits, excavating. And what happened that night was they were working in this area down here [on map]. They had heavy machinery here that they were using to dig. They had their pickup trucks that they were, you know, transporting themselves around. And they had a small mobile home where they would spend the night.

They were a crew that was out of Dallas area. Eight of them. All Anglo gentlemen. And what happened was, after the experience happened to them, which I'm going to describe, they left the work site and ran past where we are now, out to Farm to Market Road 490. And they stood by the road, trying to wave down the passing cars. And it was then that somebody contacted the Sheriff's Department. George Rapp was a dispatcher that night, and he dispatched out Joe Ponce's dad, Deputy Milo Ponce, who was a sheriff's deputy at that time. It was like the middle of the night, right, Joe?

PONCE: About 12 midnight.

TORRES: So, about midnight. This is a picture of the primary witness in this case, the one who took all the reports from the witnesses. Deputy Milo Ponce, who later became a Hidalgo County commissioner -- very well known in the area. There's a park named after him, and a lot of people still remember him as being, you know, a heavyweight in the area.

So, what happened next? As I mentioned that around midnight, Milo Ponce received this call. Do you recall, Joe? It woke you up?

PONCE: The way the house was situated, my dad's room was right here [hand gesture], and I was right next door. I mean, right in the next room. And when my dad got the phone call, it was the only phone in the house back in those days. He got the phone call. I could hear the conversation.

TORRES: The call woke up the family, and Joe says that they only had one phone and they could overhear what was being said by the dispatcher. He [Deputy Ponce] was told that a group of disturbed men and that was a term that the dispatcher used, were standing along [Farm to Market Road] 490, north of Edinburg, near Laguna Seca Road. That was the initial dispatch out to this area.

PONCE: When he got here, he found eight men standing by the side of the road in a state of great agitation. He did not at that point know what was going on. He just knew that they were very upset. They had been through something obviously traumatic. They were yelling and screaming for help, and that's what apparently caused a motorist to call it into the Sheriff's Department from a local truck stop.

TORRES: When I interviewed Joe about this a few years ago, he told me when his father received a phone call from the Sheriff's Department, he heard him asking George Rapp, the dispatcher, if it was serious or if it was a prank call. Rapp told him that the men seen along the Highway 490 were very frightened about something they had seen, and they also said they needed help putting out a fire because by that point the fire that resulted from this incident was just raging out of control.

PONCE: My father got dressed, got in his vehicle, and responded to the call. So, there's a series of gravel pits that were being worked here in that area. And when we walked down there, you're going to see, you know, several places where excavations have happened.

TORRES: The men all told the same story. In fact, what is notable to me, and I remember when Joe first brought me out here and showed me. He told me that these were hard, roughneck, construction worker types, and yet one of the men had become so upset and frightened that he had actually urinated on himself. So that was the extent to which the fright was that night.

The men were taken to the Sheriff's Office, where they were interviewed. And then they refused to go back to the work site. In fact, they insisted on leaving South Texas as soon as possible. They left the next day right away. They were allowed to spend the night at the Sheriff's Office. They told the sheriff's deputies and anybody there at the station that would listen, that they were never going to return out here, and they would never be back ever again. They supposedly left town the next day, much to their relief. They were very happy to have escaped with their lives.

So, the other interesting thing, and of course I've written a few books about UFOs, so I keyed into this right away is that the workers had told the deputies that they saw bright lights in the area before this night. And that they heard a loud humming or throbbing sound. They also had the strange phenomenon where it seemed that there was a sudden gust of wind, and there was just suddenly like a storm that was happening -- only here.

Only here in this immediate area. Nowhere else in the surrounding area.

And then the really interesting part is suddenly there was a beam of light or fire that came out of the sky and burned everything at the construction site. While these guys were fleeing the area, it just burned all their machinery to a crisp. It burned the RV in which they were staying. The mobile home. It burned their pickup trucks. Everything was just totally destroyed, basically. And Joe, you came out with your dad, right? And you want to describe what you saw?

PONCE: The following day I came out here with my dad and we came in through the main gate, which is down in this area [indicates map]. Back here behind that caliche pit -- we're right here. And the caliche pit is here, and the main gate of the old ranch.

TORRES: This is the old ranch, right?

PONCE: This was the main gate right here. I don't know if y'all can see it. The main gate is right here. It's up behind the street back there. And the area that is back that way.

Men Sought Help

Caliche Pit

Work Site

Old Gate

Area of Fire

UFO Lights
Seen Hovering Here
Moving West to East

PONCE: Between these two areas is where most of the fire was. Including some of this field right here was charred. And when we got out here the following day, the fire was already out. But you could see the amount of damage that was left behind by whatever had caused it. And they were talking about what had happened that night, and I could hear the conversation between my father and some other investigators over there -- deputies, and they were talking about what had happened that night. It sounded like something that was farfetched. But it really had happened because the evidence was out there.

Ponce (right) points to the extent of the fire.

TORRES: Very good. Thank you. One of the interesting things about this incident is that Joe told me that later on the sheriff at the time received a visit from some gentlemen in military uniforms who told them that they wanted to contain the story and not let anybody know.

And Joe says that his dad after that never told anybody this story ever again for the rest of his life.

When we visited here, about four or five years ago … that was before some of the improvements that have been made since then were made… this is what it looked like, and I want to show you some of the pieces that Joe and I found out there that day. We found the pieces of sheet metal and so forth that had indications that they had been in a fire. And they were all, you know, rusty, because it's been close to fifty years ago. So, we found a lot of this stuff out there, and it's still out there when we go out there. We were out there earlier doing that, and we found some pieces that we laid out on the ground. We're going to show it to you, those of you that are coming with us. We also found rocks that had evidence of being charred.

PONCE: What I can remember about that night was that my dad received a phone call from the Sheriff's Department at around 12 midnight. And the dispatcher, who at that time was George Rapp, was telling my dad to get out here to this area because there were some people that were standing out on Highway 490 and they were asking for help, and they were acting kind of particular. And my dad came out here. And that's when he found these gentlemen out here…. And the people that were standing out here asking for help were the workers that were working in the ranch and the caliche. That's getting caliche out. They worked for a company from upstate. They were all Anglo gentlemen. And that's when my father describes one, in particular, a gentleman who had just his T-shirt on and his pants. But he had urinated all over himself. That's how scared he was.

TORRES: He must have seen something really unusual. And they refused to go back to the work site after this.

PONCE: Right. Yes, they ended the report -- if you ever find that police report -- in the report, it says that Mr. Gonzalez had asked them to go back, you know, to where they were staying, and they refused. They refused to go back. They weren't going to do it. They didn't have just one occasion to see whatever they had seen [the UFO], but they had seen it several times.

TORRES: That's a very interesting thing. This area already at that time had a tradition for strange sightings of balls of light known as orbs and other things have been seen here in the area. In fact, there was a local resident ... Joe and I went out there earlier. And he pointed out to me that there's, like, a two-story house in a new subdivision back there that's about where this gentleman used to live. Right, Joe? Way back then. His name was Manito. And he reported seeing a cigar shaped object that hovered over the field that night, and Joe can, when we get down there, Joe can point out the field where Manito saw that. And he had seen other bright lights hovering over the surrounding fields.

So they called these ... what's really interesting is Joe says they called these La Luz del Campo. That's how they referred to these strange lights that were seen here at night. Which in English means the light of the fields. The local people at that time would say that they saw these all the time.

The UFO Site

So, it's like, you know, how many of you have heard of the Marfa Lights? Well, this is like the Edinburg lights, and they used to be seen here all the time -- so yeah. Very interesting.

Now this is the part that really blows my mind. Joe Ponce says that Sheriff Vickers told his dad that he'd been approached by two men dressed in military uniforms, asking to see the report about the incident.

Vickers, you know, was the sheriff at that time and lived in Donna. Vickers thought the men might have come from Moore Air Base. Which you know may or may not have been accurate because Moore Air Base at that time was not an Air Force installation officially, although it was still a federal compound. Nobody was allowed to go on it. So, they may have been from Moore Air Base or may have been from another base.

So, this is the quote and I remember this quote distinctly that Joe gave me. No more was ever said of the incident, and my father never spoke about it anymore. So, that is how much of an impression those military men made. Now we're going to have to ask Nick Redfern about this, because this fits the category of the men in black. So, even though they were dressed in military uniforms, their tactics were similar to the men in black. Nick Redfern, who will be one of our speakers on Saturday, is an expert on the men in black.

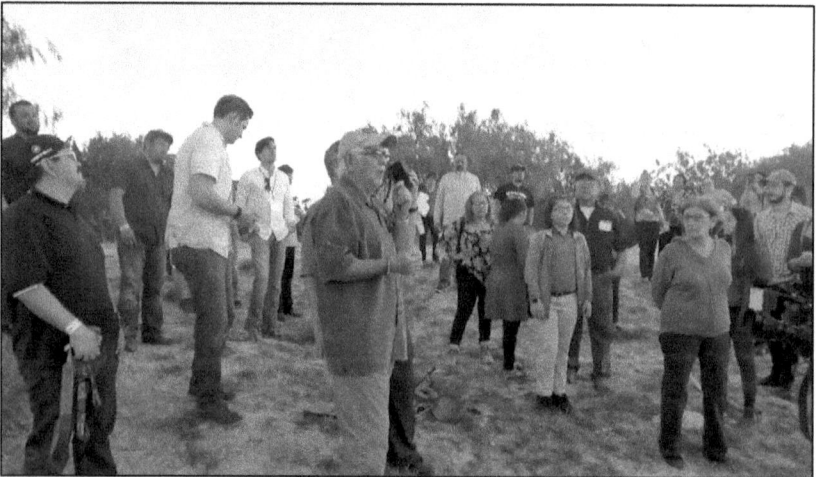

Jose J. Ponce (middle) speaks to the group at the UFO site.

Many of you probably don't realize that nuclear materials were kept here at Moore Air Base. In the 1950s, it has been revealed through the Freedom of Information Act and through other sources that the government, the Atomic Energy Commission, had approved the transfer of nuclear materials to Moore Air Base prior to the Screwworm Eradication Program.

We know that for the screwworms they use limited amounts of laboratory quantities of radioactive materials in the worms, but this was used before there was radioactive materials kept here. Now we know that in the UFO field, there seems to be a correlation between the presence of nuclear materials, especially nuclear weapons, and sightings of UFOs. For whatever reason, we're not certain. So interestingly, in the document releases that have been made, here we have confirmed that there were nuclear materials stored at Moore Air Base and contaminated materials were later buried in and around Moore Air Base. In fact, there was a huge cleanup of radioactive materials conducted just in the year 2008.

So right there at the base, which, by the way, is off limits to you and me, the Taxpayers. Cannot go in there. They'll stop you at the gate. And so, the role of Moore Air Base is very, very interesting. As I mentioned earlier, there's been some interesting incidents that happened there and there's a lot more we could say about more events, but I'm just going to close with this. So, we can go on our walk.

This is a quote from a local gentleman who's lived here his entire life and was familiar with some of the pilots who flew out of Moore Air Base, David Newton. He says we have an area that has been noted for strange

lights, frequently mentioned by both trainers and trainees in Moore Field.

When it was an advanced pilot training facility for
the US Air Force. This is in the 50s. We knew of various
such trainers and other Air Force personnel who lived in
McAllen and would mention the odd moving lights.
When they were on night training missions, these men,
frequently combat veterans from World War II or Korea,
would suggest at times that they felt as if they were being
monitored by intelligently operated craft of unknown
origin. Sometimes during the day, but mostly at night.

[Audience re-convenes at the UFO site.]

TORRES: Here in 1966, there was a strange incident
that happened. Here were eight construction workers
from the Dallas area that suddenly saw this beam of light
or fire come down out of the sky, and it totally destroyed
their construction site. It burned to a crisp, their pickup
trucks, their construction machinery, their heavy equipment. And the small RV where they were spending the
nights out here.

View of the UFO site, along an edge.

What they first heard was what sounded like a storm, but it was concentrated right here in this area only. I mean, it was perfect weather that evening throughout the area. But in this one place, there was a sudden gust of wind and something like a strong storm happened.

They ran outside, scared, and that's when they saw this beam of light come out of the sky. They took off running toward the Farm to Market 490. And what happened was everything caught fire, and many years later we're still finding little pieces of metal that we think were related to what happened that night.

In fact, all around this area, you're going to find little pieces of metal like this [showing a piece]. They show evidence of being burned, rusted out, as you walk around the old caliche pit. You can pick up these fragments pretty liberally anywhere, and then we also have rocks like this one that shows signs of being, you know, totally blackened. You know, there's ash on it. And there's a lot of these in the area as well.

So, this is an unexplained incident that happened here in Edinburg back in 1966. The gentleman from the Sheriff's Department, the deputy that responded that night and interviewed those eight construction workers, was Joe Ponce's dad.

TWELVE: 2022 WALKING TOUR

THE CITY OF EDINBURG PRESENTS

EDINBURG UFO FESTIVAL 2022

As part of the 2022 Edinburg UFO Festival, the organizers hosted a barbecue at the former Sam Gonzalez Ranch and, for the first time since 2017, offered a walking tour to any member of the general public interested in seeing where the 1966 Edinburg UFO Incident happened. Author Noe Torres acted as the emcee for the event, along with Daniel Alan Jones. Prior to the walking tour, Jose J. Ponce once again told the amazing story about the UFO encounter that he and his dad experienced. The following is a transcript of Ponce's comments, with only very slight editing for grammar and continuity.

TORRES: Just quickly want to mention that back when we first found out about this story, Joe [Ponce] came forward and told us about what happened with his dad. I believe that was 2012 time frame, Joe, but since then the story has really spread and we notice that it's being covered by more and more media.

We've had a lot of folks from the UFO community that have been down here to look over the location over the years, and we've had a lot of media coverage both about the festival and about the incident that happened in 1966. It's becoming more and more well known, as opposed to originally nobody knew about it.

The Edinburg Festival was recently ranked number three among the top ten UFO festivals in the world. Of course, we believe we're number one. And the most recent thing is I was recently asked to take part in a show that might include information about the Edinburg incident. It's going to be a second season episode of *UFO Witness*. It features Ben Hansen, who's been a speaker here with us several times, and so that show is coming up. I gave him the information, Joe, as best I could.

And as far as new developments, there's a couple of things I'd like to mention before Joe speaks. Last time we talked about the military jacket which we have back there. You can look at it afterwards. We had a group of researchers come with equipment, and they took readings all around. While there was no significant radioactivity, they found there was some strange electromagnetic signal interference that they picked up, especially as they moved their equipment close to some of the debris. There's debris all over the site, by the way.

Jose J. Ponce speaks at the 2022 Walking Tour.

Before we go walking down there, I'm going to give you all some warnings. Because it can be hazardous, but we'll get into that later. Also, after we spend about 20 or 30 minutes down there, those of us, all those of you that are going on the walking tour will come back here for the last part of our program, which is "UFO Untold Stories." We ask that if you have questions about what happened with the UFO incident, you can ask them at that time after we return to this location.

All right, so I'm going to ask Joe, because he was a firsthand witness, and he was here with his dad when this happened. Joe, if you wouldn't mind just taking us through the whole thing from the time that your dad received the initial dispatch. And all the way through to when he arrived at the scene, saw those men, and then when you became involved in witnessing what happened. So, ladies and gentlemen, here is Joe Ponce.

PONCE: Hello, my name is Joe Ponce. And I've been a lifelong resident of Edinburg, Texas. My dad, his name is J. R. Milo Ponce -- older people might know who he was. But I'm going to start with the incident that took place, and this was sometime around October or November of 1966. The reason I remember that is because that was my senior year in high school. And so, in reference to what happened that night, I was asleep, and it was around 12 midnight. My bedroom in the house happened to be right next to my mom and dad's room. There was a little hallway, and the telephone was up against the wall.

If somebody started talking on the telephone, you could hear it from one room to the other. That night, the telephone rang late at night. It was probably around 12 midnight, and it was the dispatcher from the Sheriff's Department. His name was George Rapp. He was trying to tell my dad that there was an incident going on at FM 490, which is here on this road.

He was telling dad that there were some men out there, and they were acting very funny, very particular. My dad at first didn't take the incident to be serious, and he asked George if this was a joke or if this was some kind of, you know, something going on that that wasn't that important. But George insisted that somebody had telephoned the Sheriff's Department, and they had seen some gentlemen that were standing out in the middle of 490, and they were out there flagging down people or trying to get some help.

Jose J. Ponce speaks at the 2022 Walking Tour.

My dad talked to George for a few minutes, and then he told him, "Okay, I'll get dressed, and I'll go out there and check it out. So, he left, and I didn't see my dad until the morning.

According to my dad, he had come out here and he had met these gentlemen that were out here, and they were all scared. They were gentlemen who were Anglo, and they were working in the caliche. It seems that this was a very big area where there was a lot of caliche activity going on.

And my dad said that the men were very agitated. They were very excited. That they apparently had seen something [that frightened them], because some of them were so scared that one of them had even urinated in his pants. So that's how scared they were.

My dad continued to talk with them. And he went ahead and took them to the Sheriff's Department. But before that happened, there was a fire that was taking place, and the fire was covering a large area. Out here to this area back here.

They called the fire department, and the fire department came out here. I don't know how long it took the fire department to get here. But they got out here, and they were able to help with the fire.

Later on, after they had things settled down, my dad related that he went ahead and took the gentlemen to the Sheriff's Department at the county courthouse. The entrance to the Sheriff's Department was on the west side of the building. And so, he took them in and interviewed them. He took a statement down from each one of them. Those statements remained in the Sheriff's Department. And they were then given to the sheriff.

Later on, along the following day in the morning, when I walked into the bathroom, my dad came by and said that he wanted me to go with him to see something. I said, "Yeah," and got ready to go.

We entered the ranch over by the old gate, down there…. Here was where most of the blaze had taken place. This is where my dad stated that the gentlemen had seen a strange light that had come down and was hovering over them, and that apparently the light -- or something that came from the light -- set the place on fire.

The people that lived around here.... Before the incident had taken place, they had seen those strange lights. And they had seen some strange, I guess, objects in the sky, whatever you want to call them.

I remember a local gentleman rode up on his horse while we were looking at all the burned stuff. He asked what had happened, and dad related to him what had happened. The horse rider said, "Oh, this was one of them. We see them all the time."

According to my dad, later on he said that all the Sheriff Department information that they had taken now was picked up by two gentlemen in military uniforms. Not in black suits or whatever. They were in military uniform.

TORRES: I remember you saying that your dad was basically told never to speak about this again.

PONCE: Yeah, there was another gentleman who was in charge. His name was Tom Wingert, and Mr. Wingert advised that the people that came out here told everyone not to speak about the incident. And so that's why they never spoke about it except for that one day that I happened to be here.

TORRES: Your dad never spoke about it to anyone other than you?

PONCE: My dad never related the story to anybody, you know, because he, being a former military man and also [later] being a captain on the Highway Patrol and a county commissioner..."

TORRES: We appreciate it very much, Joe. It's an amazing story. And before we walk down and do a quick tour of where this all happened, we just have a few caveats. A few warnings. I also wanted to mention a little bit about Moore Air Base, which is just down the road from here. It was a primary pilot training center for the US Air Force until 1959. And even though it was not an active military installation in 1966, the military was still using it and landing aircraft there.

I have spoken to personnel who worked in the screwworm eradication program in the 1960s, and they said that they would take all the employees of the screwworm plant, and they would make them go indoors because these big military aircraft would land late at night. There were men that would exit from those craft carrying containers. And they didn't know exactly what was going on, and they weren't supposed to know....

All right, as we go on our walking tour, I have some important things to share with you. We did some filming there this morning. We asked folks to bring sturdy footwear -- and of course those of you that are already here with what you have on, but we want you to look out for large thorns. There are some rusty strands of barbed wire. On the ground in random locations, there's metallic debris all over, especially on the outside ring of the caliche pit. We recommended that you not bring flip flops, open toed shoes or thin-soled footwear. Those of you that want to walk down to the site but not go down into the pit, that's probably safer if you have those type of shoes. Pants are preferable because there's a lot of thorny bushes down there. There's a lot of metallic debris. There are twisted pieces of metal, very rusty. We ask that you be extremely careful around it. Be careful not to step on any of that, and don't try picking any of that up.

We ask that you do not remove any items from the grounds as this is a protected site that is still under research. We still have UFO researchers coming out here and looking into what happened. Watch out for loose rocks. It's very easy to slip and turn an ankle. The barbed wire strands and lots of pits and holes. The whole thing is an uneven, walking surface, so be careful.

There are, of course, occasionally I know... Mary and her family... occasionally you see snakes, right? Rattlers. We didn't see any this morning during the filming, thank goodness. But keep an eye out for snakes, scorpions, and any other potentially hazardous critters.

Does anyone have any questions? Any questions? Once we get down there, you're free to take pictures. Look around. We do have a time frame. Because we have to go on to the next part of our program in about 20 to 30 minutes. All right. So everybody follow us.

THIRTEEN:
2019 OPEN MIC

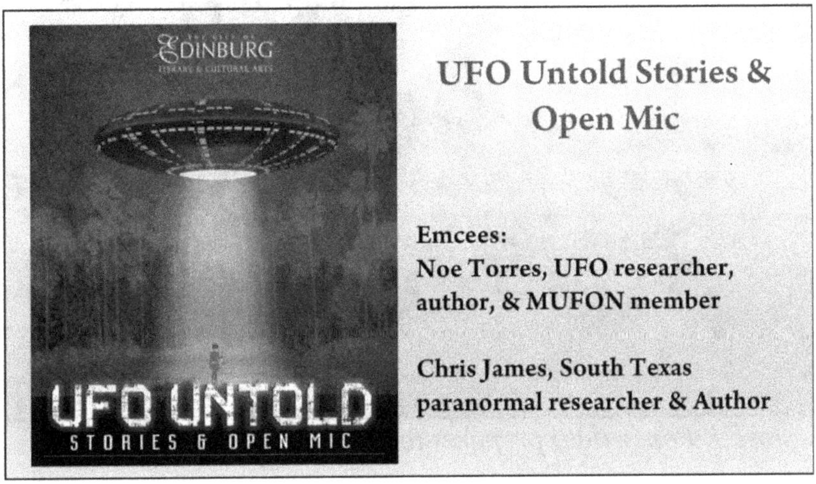

EDINBURG
UFO UNTOLD
STORIES & OPEN MIC
UFO Untold Stories & Open Mic
Emcees:
Noe Torres, UFO researcher, author, & MUFON member
Chris James, South Texas paranormal researcher & Author

On April 4, 2019, Jose J. Ponce once again told the amazing story of the Edinburg UFO Incident, this time during a program called “UFO Untold Stories & Open Mic,” held at the Edinburg City Auditorium. What follows is the transcript of Ponce’s comments, with only minor editing for grammar and continuity.

TORRES: [to Joe Ponce] Come on up if you don't mind, and I'm going to be asking for your input as we tell this story. There were eight construction workers that were basically excavating in a caliche pit out at that location, the Sam Gonzalez ranch back in 1966. The date as Joe remembers it was either October or November, and it happened at about midnight. And I'm going to have Joe come up and talk about it. His dad was there, became involved in the story when he first heard from the dispatcher and what he saw when he first got out to the location.

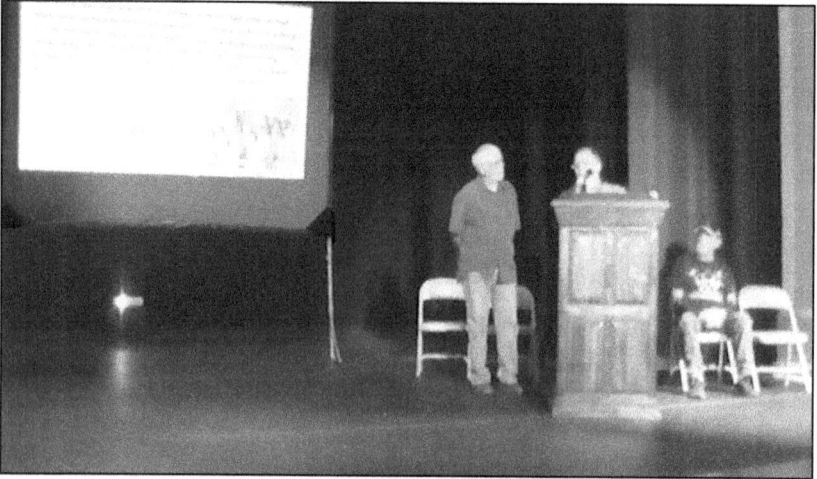

Jose J. Ponce (left) prepares to speak at the 2019 Open Mic.

PONCE: The story that you see here on the screen happened sometime around, as best I can remember, November or October 1966.

Well, my dad was deputy sheriff at the time for Hidalgo County. My father received a phone call, and it was roughly around 12 midnight when the call came in. My room was adjacent to my father in the house. At that time, we were living on 18th [Avenue] and Fay. 18th is now Veterans Boulevard.

I remember my dad talking to the dispatcher. He was asking the dispatcher for more information -- if what he was telling him was real … what he was talking about. And the dispatcher told him that yes, you have to go out there and respond.

The call was about some gentlemen who were working out there at that time, and these gentlemen were working out of there at a caliche pit. They were from somewhere in North Texas and were all Anglos. So, they were alongside Farm to Market Road 490, and they seemed to be highly excited. They were nervous.

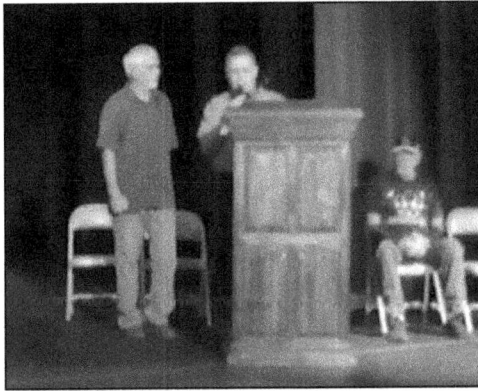

They were scared. And in fact, one of the gentlemen who my father contacted was so scared that he had urinated on himself.

I remember my dad preparing to leave the house to go on this call. I remember him leaving the house in his car, going north on 18th street. I could see the little red light on top of his car. I don't know how long it took him to get out there.

But when he got out to the location, sure enough they [the construction workers] were there. They were all scared. They said they had seen something and couldn't explain it. They didn't want to state [what they had seen].

My dad went ahead and took the gentleman back to the Sheriff's Department, and they stayed there overnight. The following day they left. There was a report filed.

Artist's Conception (Pixabay)

The fire department also went out to the same location because of the fire that had come out of the sky.

My father was speaking to somebody about what happened. Apparently, these gentlemen … it was a calm night. It was a very calm night. And for some reason or other there was a loud, strong wind that came up on the trailer house where they were staying there at the job location.

Dad said the wind was so strong that it made. a humming sound, or a pulsating sound. What happened next was they said that out of that thing [UFO] they saw in the sky, there seemed to be some kind of beam of some kind. There was like a spot that came out of it, and that's what caused the fire at the location.

My father said that the gentleman said they would not return to Edinburg because of that reason.

If I can remember right the sheriff at that time was E. E. Vickers, and the assistant chief was Tom Wingert, and they told the story that during the same period of time after that took place, maybe the following day, I'm not too sure, these people showed up in military uniforms, and they wanted to either speak [about] or see the report. Shortly thereafter, the men in uniforms left, and the incident was never spoken about. It was never told again. It was told in stories, like among friends when you talk about crazy things that can't be explained.

It wasn't just the sheriff's department that had seen these [UFOs] in the sky. Some people [around the Sam Gonzalez Ranch] say they had seen a light that used to appear in the open fields, north of the ranch house.

And these fields were probably a couple hundred acres in length, maybe longer. There were ranches to the east and ranches to the west. And all of these people that lived out there in the 1960s all reported basically the same thing -- that late at night or sometimes in the early evening, they would see these strange lights in the sky. And apparently that night when the incident occurred, there were strange lights in the sky.

Artist's Conception (Pixabay)

And one man who happened to live out at a ranch -- he was the foreman of the ranch. His name was Manito.

And when they asked him about the lights and what he had seen, he simply said that what he had seen was an object that appeared to be cigar shaped, and it was illuminated, and he said that it would light up the field. And it would light up the neighboring brush line... But anyway, on this night, Manito said the lights had been there that night."

Staff of Project Blue Book, 1960s USAF Investigators of UFOs

I wasn't there the night of the incident, only the officers and the fire department, but the following day I showed up there and was able to see some of the stuff that was burned out there – it was burned real, real bad. I have never seen anything like it. It was just there. It was charred. Everything was charred. And we looked around for a while, at everything there.

TORRES: This is such a fascinating story. Every time I heard you tell your dad mentioned that some guys in Air Force uniforms showed up, and they were pretty serious.

PONCE: Yeah, the two gentlemen that showed up in military uniforms. They wanted to see everything. The report. They wanted to talk to the people that had actually done the investigation. And I'm more than sure they spoke with my dad and with all the people involved.

TORRES: What's really interesting is we had a really hard time tracking down any documents, any supporting documents. And I'm sure Nick Pope could speak to this. My theory is that they made everything disappear. Those guys from the Air Force.

PONCE: I've been doing, and I've been trying to find somebody that probably will have some kind of documentation, which may still be out there.

TORRES: Interesting angle and research into the role that Moore Air Base may have had in this. You know Moore Air Base is located only about 5 air miles from where this happened, and over the years, Moore Air Base has been the site of many local mysteries. I don't know if you were aware of this.

All along the flight paths that the pilots were coming in and out of Moore Air Base, there were also reports of strange craft that did not appear to be conventional. They did not appear to be modern jets, and so it is interesting to me, even to this day, reports of strange objects hovering around Moore Air Base. There are still reports coming into local investigators.

So, what's fascinating to me is that this ranch is where this incident happened so close to Moore Air Base.

Stephen Bassett, who was one of our speakers last year, came up with a theory. We're standing out there looking -- we were showing him around the site, and he said, you know, it may not have been a fire that came down from the object. It may have been some kind of spontaneous reaction to whatever energy was driving that craft. In other words, [it may have been caused by] the energy from the craft that might have disseminated down to all the metal objects that were on the ground and set them all ablaze.

Stephen Bassett During Visit to Edinburg in 2018

It could have been something to do with the propulsion system of the craft or some kind of energy from that strange craft. We don't know if they've been testing strange objects out of Moore Air Base, which is a, quote - unquote, retired US Air Force Base, which is now supposedly under the domain of the US Department of Agriculture. But if any of you go out there to look around, they won't let you. There are armed guards that tell you to go away. No trying to take any pictures from inside the big fence that covers the whole thing.

But anyway, the other interesting thing we found out, Joe, and I know you weren't aware of this, is there were radioactive materials kept by the US Air Force since the 1950s, so much so that the government had to recently do a major abatement of radioactive materials at that base. Local journalists were taking pictures of these guys in what looked like spacesuits, walking around the compound, digging up radioactive materials.

After last year's conference, a person who worked many years at Moore Air Base in the Screwworm Eradication Program said yes, the US Agriculture Department had control of that base in the 60s, 70s, 80s, but strange aircraft would land there all the time, and they would tell the screwworm employees to move away from the landing fields and go into a building without windows while these planes landed and took out whatever cargo they had.

But on one occasion he said he managed to see one of these strange aircraft from the Air Force land. And you have these men in biohazard suits carrying boxes, he said. Hey, we don't know exactly what was going on, but he [the witness] knew that the government was using Moore Air Base for something other than just the screwworm eradication program.

FOURTEEN: EDINBURG INCIDENT GOES VIRAL

Jose J. Ponce's revelation in 2012 about the Edinburg UFO incident led to a discussion about having an annual town festival related to UFOs. As it turned out, the idea was a success, and the Edinburg UFO Conference & Festival, which started in 2012 continues yearly as of the writing of this book (2023).

Before committing to having an annual festival, author Noe Torres was asked to hold a lecture about UFOs at the Dustin Sekula Memorial Library in Edinburg on

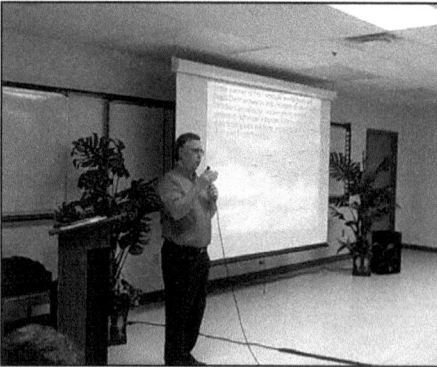

the evening of January 12, 2012. To an enthusiastic, standing room only crowd of over 200 people, Torres gave a presentation called "UFOs Over Texas," an overview of fascinating cases that had occurred mostly in the Rio Grande Valley and South Texas. The success of this one event provided proof that residents of Edinburg and surrounding communities were highly interested in hearing more about this fascinating topic. It provided the impetus for the city's library and cultural activities personnel to begin planning for the town's first official, annual UFO conference, to be held on Friday, August 10, 2012, in the Edinburg City Auditorium.

Shortly after the events described above, Torres proposed to library director Letty Leija the concept of having an annual UFO-related festival along the lines of the Roswell UFO Festival, where Torres had been a featured speaker for five years (2007-2012). Still uncertain if the concept was viable, the library staff decided to have a "mini conference" in August 2012, as an evening event, featuring only three speakers, Torres, Dr. Robert Gross of the Mutual UFO Network (MUFON), and paranormal investigator Ismael Cuellar of Laredo.

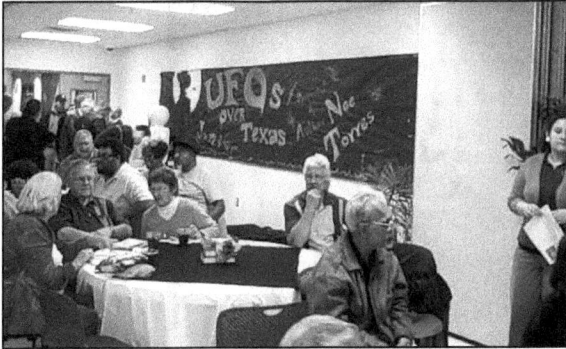

The first "official" Edinburg UFO Conference was therefore held on Friday, August 10, 2012, in the Edinburg City Auditorium, and again, the public response was overwhelming with over 500 people attending. Torres spoke on "UFOs over South Texas," while Cuellar spoke on "South Texas UFO Hunters," and Gross talked about the "Kecksburg (Pennsylvania) UFO Incident." Attendees were extremely happy with the mini-conference, and momentum began to build toward having a full-scale UFO conference / festival sometime in the spring of 2013.

EDINBURG UFO CONFERENCE

Date: Friday, August 10, 2012
Time: 6 P.M. - 8 P.M.
Location: City Auditorium
415 W. University - Edinburg, TX

Special Presenters:
Dr. Robert Gross
Noe Torres
Ismael Cuellar

Afterwards join us for Jardín del Arte in the City Hall Courtyard

Presented By:

For more information contact Jose Tanez at 956-383-6246 or visit us on the web at www.edinburgarts.com

The stage was set to hold the full-scale Edinburg "Out of This World!" UFO Conference & Festival (2nd annual) on March 15, 2013, featuring several of the world's top UFO speakers, including nuclear physicist Stanton Friedman of Canada and UFO abductee Travis Walton, whose abduction was the basis for the Hollywood movie *Fire in the Sky*.

Because of the anticipated larger crowd, the event was moved to the Edinburg Conference Center at Renaissance, an ultra-modern, high-tech facility that has hosted world-class speakers and performers. The 2013 event was another major success, attracting hundreds of spectators to the Edinburg Conference Center at Renaissance, where the audience enjoyed a full day of multimedia presentations related to the UFO phenomenon.

2013 Guest Speakers: L-R, Stanton Friedman, Noe Torres, and Travis Walton.

Shown above are the 2013 speakers: Ismael Cuellar (rightmost), Noe Torres (2nd from right), Stanton Friedman (3rd from right), Travis Walton (4th from left), Dr. Bob Gross (2nd from left), and Stephen Andrasko (leftmost).

Stanton Friedman (left) and Noe Torres (right) during interview with KURV Radio about 2013 Conference.

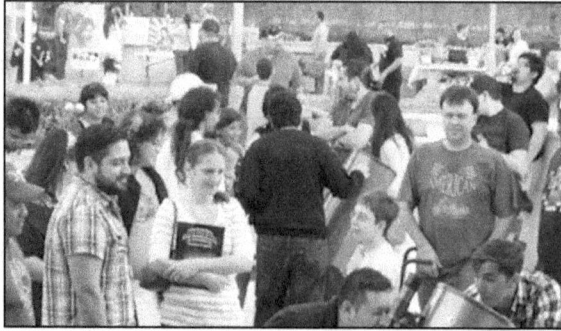

Photo taken at the first outdoor UFO Festival
held on March 15, 2013.

As soon as the 2013 event ended, planning began for 2014, with the date moved from March to June. Speakers were invited to present about two of the world's best known UFO incidents – the Roswell UFO crash, which was addressed by award-winning author Dr. Kevin Randle, and the Betty & Barney Hill abduction, which was addressed by Betty Hill's niece, Kathleen Marden, a UFO abduction expert. The 2014 event was again extremely well attended, and plans were immediately announced to have another conference & festival in 2015.

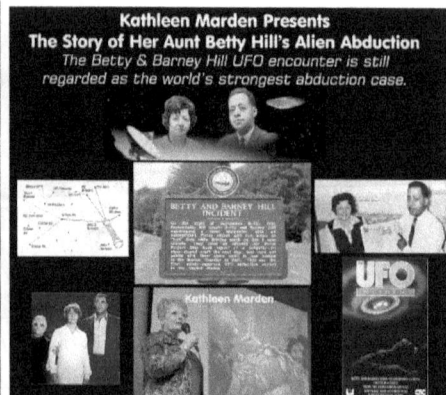

Still trying to find the best time of year to hold the event, organizers moved it to August in 2015. Riding the wave of enthusiasm from the first three events, the 2015 conference & festival featured the world's best known paranormal radio talk show host, George Noory of the extremely popular "Coast to Coast AM with George Noory" and brought to Edinburg a celebrity from the world of show business, Mark Goddard, who played Major Don West on the hit 1960s television series "Lost in Space." At the UFO festival on Friday night, August 14, the lines were huge to meet and get autographs from Mr. West and the other speakers. By the time the 2015 festival came around, the Edinburg event was becoming firmly established in the Rio Grande Valley as an annual event that was worthy of public attention. The event was also starting to receive recognition on a national and global scale as an important paranormal-themed event.

A few months after the 2015 event, during the annual "State of the City" address, Edinburg mayor Richard Garcia acknowledged the increasing importance of the

UFO conference & festival, saying, "Edinburg has invested millions of dollars to increase cultural arts opportunities in the form of performing arts, live performances and festivals, such as the South Texas International Film Festival and the ever-popular UFO Annual Conference."

Edinburg Mayor Richard Garcia Recognizes the Role of the UFO Conference in May 2016

In 2016, the conference & festival remained in the month of August and brought in as featured speakers David Childress of the hit television series *Ancient Aliens*,

Ben Hansen of *Fact or Faked: Paranormal Files*, Dr. Lynne Kitei of *The Phoenix Lights*, and authors Nick Redfern and Noe Torres.

Attendance was again very high both for the free Friday evening festival and for the Saturday conference. It was the fifth success in a row for the Edinburg event, and recognition was spreading.

In April 2017, despite one of the originally scheduled speakers becoming critically ill and being unable to attend at the last minute, it ended up being one of the most successful and well-attended editions in the event's history. With Texan UFO researchers Darrel Sims and Nick Redfern filling in at the last minute for the ailing Jim Marrs, who unfortunately passed away a few months later, the Edinburg event was an unqualified success, and the recognition finally reached national and global proportions.

An extremely popular feature of the 2017 event was a lecture on site followed by a walking tour of the location where witnesses said a UFO hovered over a construction site and shot down beams of fire. This special event was discussed at length in a previous chapter of this book.

Shortly after the 2017 event wrapped, the stunning news was received that the Edinburg "Out of This World!" UFO Conference & Festival was ranked by *ListVerse.com* as #3 among the world's "Top 10 Festivals for UFO And Alien Lovers." Supporters and fans of the event were absolutely ecstatic to hear that the little event that began with a simple lecture held in the city's public library in 2012 had moved on to take an important place among the world's paranormal-themed festivals.

2018 marked the 7th year of the event, and three world-class speakers appeared, as the conference moved to the middle of April. UFO abductee Travis Walton, one of the conference's most popular speakers, returned to the event for the first time since 2013. Joining him were UFO experts Nick Pope, John Greenewald, and Stephen Bassett.

The 2019 conference & festival (8th Annual), held April 5 & 6, featured one of the most ambitious line-ups of UFO experts yet, including Donald R. Schmitt, who worked with the legendary Dr. J. Allen Hynek as one of his special investigators. A former director of the Hynek Center for UFO Studies and its director of special investigations for ten years, Schmitt is one of the world's top experts on the U.S. Air Force's "Project Blue Book" and its chief scientist (Hynek), as featured on the History Channel series "Project Blue Book."

Another featured speaker was UFO abductee Calvin Parker. On the evening of October 11, 1973, Parker and the late Charles Hickson, were fishing off a pier on the west bank of the Pascagoula River in Mississippi when they saw a brightly glowing UFO descend from the sky and hover near them.

Three unearthly beings came out of the object, paralyzed them, and took them aboard. Dr. J. Allen Hynek, the world's foremost UFO expert at the time, interviewed Parker and Hickson, concluding that the men were, "Absolutely honest. They have had a fantastic experience."

Other speakers for the 2019 conference included retired U.S. Air Force Colonel Charles Halt, a first-hand eyewitness to the world-famous Rendlesham Forest UFO encounter in 1980, UFO experts Ben Moss & Tony Angiona of the TV series *Hangar 1: UFO Files*, and paranormal researcher Nick Redfern.

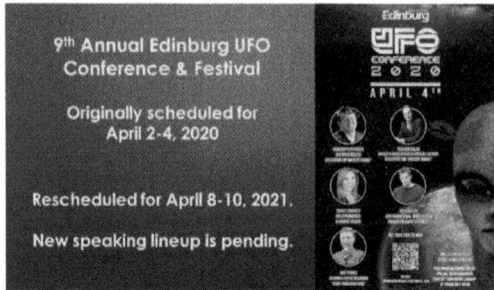

Regretfully, the 2020 Edinburg UFO Conference & Festival, like many other events throughout the world, was cancelled due to the COVID 19 pandemic. As it turned out, Edinburg and surrounding cities in South Texas were hit especially hard by the disease, and the pandemic took its toll on social gatherings.

The 2021 Festival Was Held Outdoors

In 2021, the pandemic was still affecting the area, and the festival organizers decided on a scaled-down event, to be held outdoors. The featured speakers included Nick Pope, Ben Hansen, Darrel Sims, Kevin Day, and Daniel Alan Jones. Although small, the event was well enjoyed by the attendees.

2022 was the year that the Edinburg UFO Conference & Festival returned to its pre-pandemic status, celebrating its 10th annual event. It was held in the historic Edinburg City Auditorium, the site of the very first event in 2012.

The featured speakers for 2022 were Mike Bara, Christopher O'Brien, Peter Robbins, Ken Gerhard, Noe Torres, Jane Kyle, and Daniel Jones. The attendance was once again fabulous, and fans of the conference were extremely happy to see a return to normalcy.

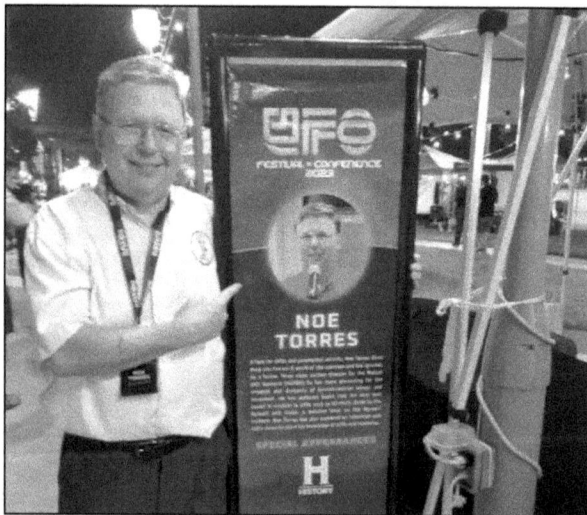

The 2023 event moved to a new venue, the Region One Education Service Center in Edinburg, and the attendance was outstanding at the new facility. Due to a number of scheduling conflicts, the event was held in August, for the first time since 2016. Speakers were David Childress, Mike Bara, Stanley Milford, Jonathan Dover, Marc D'Antonio, Noe Torres, and Daniel Alan Jones.

The Edinburg UFO Conference & Festival continues to grow in popularity each year, fueled by the amazing story that is largely responsible for inspiring it – the 1966 Edinburg UFO Incident. When eyewitness Jose J. Ponce came forward to tell his dad's remarkable story in 2012, few people could have guessed that it would set into motion one of the world's most recognized annual UFO celebrations!

Clearly, what happened in 1966 remains an extremely powerful and fascinating narrative. It is a case that merits much closer study and investigation. The author concludes with the hope that this small volume will help the story grow and will inspire further research into exactly what happened that night in 1966 at the Sam Gonzalez Ranch when a UFO broke out of a cloud bank and shot beams of fire upon a construction camp and its crew.

INDEX

UFOs of the Turbulent Thirties!!!
Now Available at RoswellBooks.com

It seems that "flying saucers" would be the farthest thing from the minds of Americans in the 1930s, and yet a new book proves otherwise. *UFOs of the Turbulent Thirties* discloses many astonishing UFO sightings that took place from 1930 – 1939, as America suffered through the Great Depression, gangsters roamed large cities, and the nation was on the verge of joining World War II.

The book by UFO researchers Noe Torres and John Lemay is the eighth in a series covering the history of American UFO sightings from the year 1800 to 1939. Although UFOs did not fully enter the public consciousness until 1947, Torres and LeMay's books have disclosed thousands of significant encounters during America's formative years.

Included in the book is the amazing story of Nazi Germany's efforts to reverse-engineer flying saucer technology and thereby conquer the world. In fact, according to the authors, the Nazis believed they were descended from extraterrestrials and were therefore entitled to exploit these advanced technologies, including experiments into time travel! Nazi experiments on rockets began in 1934.

UFO Crash on the Texas-Mexico Border
Now Available at RoswellBooks.com

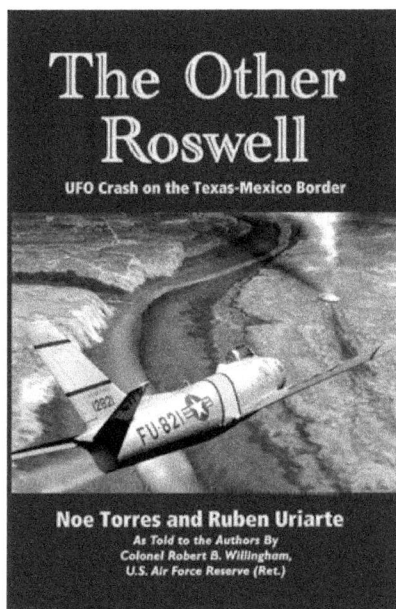

The Other Roswell

UFO Crash on the Texas-Mexico Border

Noe Torres and Ruben Uriarte

As Told to the Authors By
Colonel Robert B. Willingham,
U.S. Air Force Reserve (Ret.)

On a clear spring day in 1955, Air Force reservist Robert Willingham was piloting an F-86 fighter jet across West Texas when he saw an intensely bright UFO streak past his aircraft at over 2,000 miles per hour and then crash-land along the banks of the Rio Grande River, where he later found smoldering, twisted wreckage that convinced him the object was not of the Earth.

Dr. Bruce Maccabee, world-class UFO researcher, says about this book, "One of the world's most interesting UFO crash retrieval stories. I believe that the reader will find this book important support for the idea that Alien Flying Craft have crashed on earth and have been retrieved and covered up by the United States government."

The Other Roswell: UFO Crash on the Texas-Mexico Border discloses for the first time ever, the eyewitness testimony of Colonel Willingham, who says that he chased a UFO across Texas, saw it crash to the earth near Del Rio, Texas, and later visited the crash site.

You've heard about this amazing book on *Coast to Coast AM* with George Noory, the Jeff Rense program, and other shows we have done. Now, you can read the complete story from the eyewitness himself. Available for print and for the Kindle at RoswellBooks.com and through online retailers including Amazon.com.

RoswellBooks.com

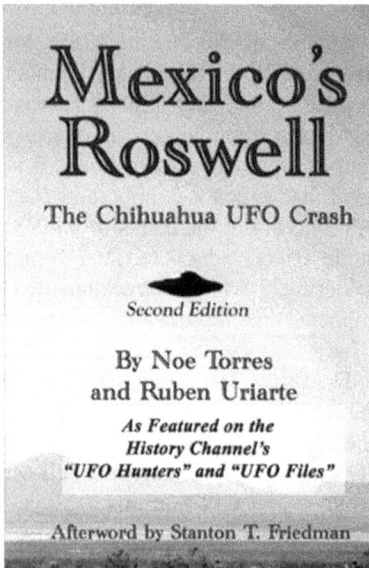

Where the Weird Things Are in Roswell!
Now Available at RoswellBooks.com

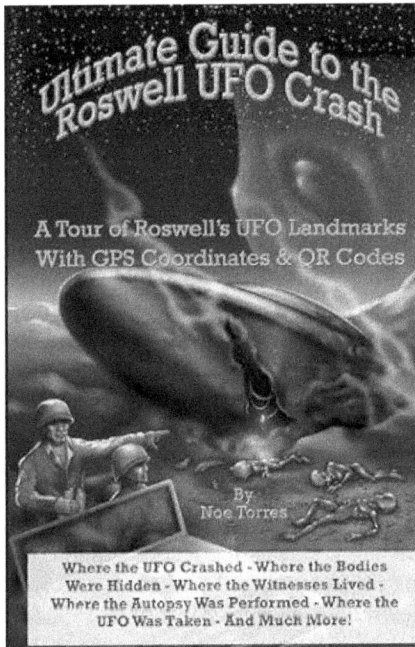

In this revised, updated edition, author Noe Torres again takes readers on an unforgettable trip back in time to July 1947, when something from beyond Earth fell out of the sky in the desert north of Roswell, New Mexico. Using historical photos, maps, and eyewitness testimony, this book takes readers on a detailed tour of the Roswell story by visiting the actual places where everything happened.Best-selling author Peter Robbins says about this book, "The Ultimate Guide is deeply informative, well illustrated and consistently interesting. This is American history most Americans are completely unaware of and a public service to anyone who wants to walk the walk and experience the Roswell story via the actual locations where it occurred. Bravo!"Veteran Roswell researcher Kevin Randle says: "If you are planning to visit Roswell, this book tells you all you need to know about the UFO crash, the city and its character. It condenses the confusion of the case into an easily read book that will help anyone make the most of a visit to city and help understand what actually happened. A very nice addition to the Roswell literature."Reviewer J. Steiger of Woodbridge, VA, said, "I read Ultimate Guide in one day. Could not put it down! This is a wonderful addition to 'Roswellicana,' and I congratulate you, Mr. Torres, on your first-rate research and scholarship."Bill Mumy, who played Will Robinson in the 1960s TV series Lost in Space, said, "Your book kept me up all night … especially the part about the alien autopsy that happened right here in Roswell."

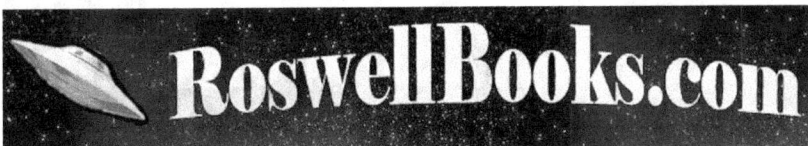

Get the Real Story of Cowboys & Aliens!
Now Available at RoswellBooks.com

Praise for our book from the *Albuquerque Journal* daily newspaper: "Hey, Hollywood. If you're going to make a big-budget movie about extraterrestrial contact with Wild West cowpunchers, can't you at least try to get it right? John LeMay, a historian and author who lives in Roswell, says that of course spacemen explored our planet in the days of saddle-sore lawmen and swinging saloon doors. But it wasn't the cartoonish picture of evil planetary invaders, complete with hideous teeth and slimy hands emanating from their reptilian bellies that are portrayed in this Hollywood blockbuster. His book ... sets the record straight, using information gathered from yellowed newspaper clippings from the 1800s to tell of numerous close encounters between farmers and cowboys on the range and mysterious visitors in flight." (*Albuquerque Journal*, Aug. 18, 2011, Page A1)

Long before graphic novels and Hollywood blockbusters, Cowboys and Aliens really did encounter each other, according to newspaper accounts and other historical documents of the 1800s. These unusual stories about UFO sightings in the Old West are revealed in a book by Texas UFO researcher Noe Torres and New Mexico historian John LeMay. This critically acclaimed book series examines bizarre incidents, including the reported recovery in 1897 of a spaceship and its alien pilot in the Texas frontier town of Aurora.

Now available for print and for the Kindle at RoswellBooks.com and through online retailers including Amazon.com.

RoswellBooks.com

www.ingramcontent.com/pod-product-compliance
Lightning Source LLC
Chambersburg PA
CBHW062102270326
41931CB00013B/3177